The Way
of the World

Crofts Classics

GENERAL EDITORS

Samuel H. Beer, *Harvard University*

O. B. Hardison, Jr., *The Folger Shakespeare Library*

WILLIAM CONGREVE

The Way of the World

EDITED BY

Henry Ten Eyck Perry

STATE UNIVERSITY OF
NEW YORK AT BUFFALO

NEW HANOVER COUNTY
PUBLIC LIBRARY
201 CHESTNUT STREET
WILMINGTON, N C 28401

AHM Publishing Corporation
Arlington Heights, Illinois 60004

Copyright © 1951
AHM PUBLISHING CORPORATION

All rights reserved

This book, or parts thereof, must not be
used or reproduced in any manner without written permission. For information
address the publisher, AHM PUB-
LISHING CORPORATION, 3110
North Arlington Heights Road, Arlington Heights, Illinois 60004.

ISBN: 0-88295-024-X
(Formerly 0-390-22107-4)

Library of Congress Card Number: 51-6756

PRINTED IN THE UNITED STATES OF AMERICA
7109
Fourteenth Printing

INTRODUCTION

THE CHIEF difficulty for readers of *The Way of the World* has always been the plot; it is extremely complicated, and its ramifications are hard to follow in detail. In the theatre it is even more difficult to straighten out than in the study, and it has no doubt contributed to the only partial success that the play has had upon the stage, from its own day to ours. So puzzling are the incidents that some critics have advised readers to forget the plot and concentrate their attention upon the dialogue, which is well known for its brilliance and polish. Unfortunately, however, to follow this last counsel is to neglect the core of the drama. Aristotle has told us that the plot, or fable, is the most important part of a good play; *The Way of the World* is such a good play that in order to appreciate it properly, it is necessary to struggle with the intricacies of its plot.

In an attempt to help the reader to do so, I have prefixed to this edition of the play an "argument," the purpose of which is to disentangle the outstanding strands in the action, after the fashion of some editions of Greek plays. As with classic dramas, much of the trouble comes from the action which has occurred before the play begins. In Greek tragedies this material was usually legendary, and knowledge of it among the audience could be taken for granted by the dramatist; in Congreve's play, the plot, which is largely original, comes as a complete surprise and has to be carefully assimilated. The technique in both cases, however, is much the same. Congreve observes a narrow conception of the unity of time, "The time equal to that of the presentation," and therefore he must employ a number of incidents which have taken place in the past and which must gradually be revealed to the audience by the conversation of the characters on the stage. My "argument of the play" is largely concerned with the confusing and complicated antecedent action.

This action is of two kinds: amatory and financial. The love affairs of the various characters are most intricate and these affairs depend to a great degree upon the economic fortunes of the persons involved in the plot. From the economic point of view Lady Wishfort is the most well-established character in the play; she holds the purse strings, and the other characters are trying in various ways to unloosen them. From the amatory point of view, Millamant is the most successful person; most of the men in the play are in love with her, and most of the women are jealous of her. Between these two women, Mirabell oscillates; his efforts to win the hand of Millamant and the £6000 of her dowry which it is in Lady Wishfort's power to dispose of constitute the principal strands of the plot. His chief scheme to accomplish this latter purpose, Waitwell's disguise as Sir Rowland, does not get under way until the fourth act. The first three acts are concerned with plans for the future and memories of the past; at the end of the fourth act Mirabell's success seems assured; between the fourth and fifth acts his plot is discovered, and he is threatened with failure; in the last act, which is filled with numerous unexpected turns of fortune, the hero finally accomplishes his purpose and wins both Millamant and her dowry. It is essential to a proper understanding of the play to be aware of the unusual but entirely logical way in which the plot is constructed.

Not only is it necessary to understand the complications of the plot, which requires strict attention and meticulous analysis, but the place of the various characters in it must constantly be kept in mind. *The Way of the World* is almost too well integrated in its construction, and it is very much like Ben Jonson's "comedy of humours" in the way the characters are handled. To read a comedy of Jonson's intelligently, one must try to keep all the characters suspended in one's mind at the same time; it sometimes seems as if the easiest thing to do would be to read the play over once for each character's part in it, putting one's attention on each figure separately and then attempting to fit together the pieces of the jig-saw puzzle into a complete and unified picture.

In *The Way of the World* there are, not counting the three servants, nine important characters, five men and four women, each of whom has a definite part in the structure of the whole play, which is so skillfully organized that it gives each of the nine a chance to display his or her own characteristics and personality. Mirabell, the motivating force in the plot, is also the most complicated individual in the cast; his combination of worldliness and good nature makes him a person whose psychology it is at times baffling to follow. He is contrasted with Fainall, who is almost all worldliness, and with Sir Wilfull Witwoud, who is almost all good nature. As a suitor to Millamant, Mirabell is opposed to Witwoud, the would-be wit, and Petulant, the ignorant pretender to social graces. He is the focal point of the love affairs in the play, since all the principal women in it are in some way attracted to him: Lady Wishfort has been flattered by his attentions and is annoyed when she finds that they were only social flattery; Mrs. Millamant loves him, as much as a fine lady of the world can love anyone but herself; Mrs. Marwood is angry that her attraction to him is not reciprocated; Mrs. Fainall has been in love with him and still likes him, in spite of the fact that he has transferred his attentions to Millamant.

Mrs. Fainall is the most contradictory and, in some ways, the most unsatisfactory person in the play. Mirabell's attitude towards her is quite clear, once one accepts the combination of ruthlessness and benevolence in his character; he is sufficiently developed by Congreve for us to come to believe in him as a possible, if not an entirely credible, character. Mrs. Fainall's psychology, on the other hand, is never fully explored. She is, like the Queen in *Hamlet*, a character about whom we would like to know more, and perhaps we do not for much the same reason that we do not know more of Queen Gertrude. They are both colorless easy-going women who accept life as it comes without struggling against it, and the dramatist has comparatively little to say about them as people. They furnish important links in the plot, but as individuals they have too little conflict within themselves to make them suitable subjects for extended consideration on the stage. Each is destroyed in the course of the action, for Mrs. Fainall's ultimate reunion with her husband, which Mirabell hints at optimistically in the last speech of the play, could only prove a fate worse than death for the unfortunate lady.

The enigmatic character of Mrs. Fainall is echoed in the ambiguity of her final position. It is apparently hoped by her friends that her loveless marriage will be patched up, so that it will conform to a conventional social pattern. That is indeed "the way of the world," which gives the play its title. The phrase occurs three times in the course of the dialogue, referring the first two times to the infidelity of wives and husbands, the last time to a happy financial outcome for the people of good will in the play. The conflict between worldliness and decency is the fundamental subject of this comedy. The usual standard of the Comedy of Manners, social elegance and grace, is here deepened to include a consideration of more basic moral values. To Congreve it is indispensable, but not enough, that people should be ladies and gentlemen; they must be admirable human beings as well. The people who are chiefly worldly, like Fainall and Mrs. Marwood, the "villains" of the piece, are routed and disgraced. The people of good will, like Sir Wilfull and Lady Wishfort (for Lady Wishfort is basically good-natured in spite of her sharp tongue and ridiculous aspirations for a second husband), are left outside the conventional framework by means of which life continues on the higher levels of aristocratic society. Witwoud and Petulant are merely useless decorations of the picture, "followers" not only of Millamant but of the whole social pattern which she gloriously represents.

Mirabell is the most important person in the plot of the comedy and the most carefully analyzed of its character, but he yields second place to Millamant in the sparkling duel of sex that takes place between them. Mirabell has

INTRODUCTION

had his affairs with other women and he is ready to settle
down into matrimony, if he can win a beautiful, talented,
and wealthy wife; it is notable that neither he nor Millamant faces the possibility of their marrying without having
secured all of her dowry. Millamant has had scores of
admirers. The problem for her is to find one man to whom
she can submit her personal freedom and integrity.

"The *proviso* scene" in the fourth act is justly the most
famous scene in the play, because in it is concentrated the
struggle between the individual and social conventions,
between human feeling and worldliness, which is the core
of the intellectual content of this comedy. It is characteris-
tic that Mirabell first uses the word "proviso" and that he
draws up the formal covenant with its "imprimis" and its
"items," which will prevent him from becoming "beyond
measure enlarged into a husband"; but it is Millamant who
has already subtly laid down conditions which must be
fulfilled before she "may by degrees dwindle into a wife."
She cannot bring herself definitely to accept Mirabell's
proposal until urged to do so by a third party, the com-
plaisant Mrs. Fainall, to whom she later confides, "Well,
if Mirabell should not make a good husband, I am a lost
thing; for I find I love him violently." To Mirabell himself,
however, she never makes such a straightforward admis-
sion, and the last words that we hear her say to him in the
play are the bantering, "Why does not the man take me?
Would you have me give myself to you over again?"

Whether or not Millamant loves Mirabell violently, she
loves him to a degree which is for her nothing short of violence. The fine lady, sheltered from the economic crudities
of life and surrounded by the luxuries of a sophisticated
existence, is brought into touch with ordinary humanity by
her feelings. The shock is almost too great for her social
poise to endure, and she takes refuge in a dazzling shower
of words. Congreve's genius has risen to the height of
finding language to portray Millamant's shimmering personality; his own comment on his imaginative creation is to
be found in Mirabell's gasping exclamation on Millamant's
sudden exit in the second act: "Gone! Think of you? To

think of a whirlwind, though 'twere in a whirlwind, were
a case of more steady contemplation; a very tranquillity of
mind and mansion."

Congreve gives more words to Mirabell than to Millamant, no doubt because he understands the man better
than the woman. His picture of Millamant is drawn chiefly
from the outside and records the impression created by
the woman on a man. Was Congreve thinking of Mrs. Ann
Bracegirdle, who played the part of Millamant and to
whom he was devoted during the earlier part of his life,
as Molière was no doubt thinking of his wife when he
drew the parallel character of Célimène in *Le Misanthrope?*
At any rate these two great comic dramatists were able to
view with the mind's eye the mystery of the eternal feminine as it appears to a mere man; and they were able to
clothe it in words that they intended to have spoken on
the stage by the actresses with whom they were in love.

Words are the medium of the literary artist, and of
words Congreve is a past master. His most brilliant effects
are achieved in the conversation of Millamant, his most
careful ones in the speeches of Mirabell. His variety is to
be seen in the talk of the other characters, whose language
is nicely adjusted to their personalities: Meredith has
classically described Lady Wishfort's tirades as "a flow
of boudoir billingsgate"; Sir Wilfull's outpourings are
clearly the naïve expressions of a Shropshire man in conflict with the urbanities of city life. The contrast between
Sir Wilfull and his half-brother Tony Witwoud is made
clear by their language on first encountering each other
after a long separation. Sir Wilfull ejaculates "What, sure
'tis not—yea by'r Lady, but 'tis. 'Sheart, I know not
whether 'tis or no. Yea, but 'tis, by the Wrekin," and
Witwoud replies with a fashionable oath and a distant
manner, "Odso, brother, is it you? Your servant, brother."

Witwoud's language contrasts nicely not only with that
of his bumpkin half brother but also with that of his
illiterate friend, Petulant. Witwoud proceeds by "similitudes" and subtle refinements, Petulant by incoherent and
blunt assertions, as in their dialogue about quarreling:

Petulant remarks, "If he says black's black, if I have a humour to say 'tis blue, let that pass; all's one for that. If I have a humour to prove it, it must be granted," to which Witwoud counters, "Aye, upon proof positive it must; but upon proof presumptive it only may. That's a logical distinction now." In the first act of the play, Witwoud and Petulant are seen with Mirabell and Fainall, the four men's conversation crackling with sparkle and variety. Mirabell and Fainall are the men of sense whose intelligent talk contrasts with the vain babble of the two fools of fashion.

The first act of *The Way of the World* is the men's alone, and then at the beginning of the second act we are introduced to Mrs. Fainall and Mrs. Marwood in their argument about lovers. Mrs. Fainall ruefully remarks, "If we will be happy, we must find the means in ourselves, and among ourselves. Men are ever in extremes, either doting or averse," to which Mrs. Marwood bitterly replies, "True, 'tis an unhappy circumstance of life that love should ever die before us; and that the man so often should outlive the lover. But say what you will, 'tis better to be left than never to have been loved." After this dialogue, in which the superficial attitudes of the two women are revealed, each has a conversation with one of the men. Mrs. Marwood talks to Fainall and Mrs. Fainall to Mirabell, in scenes that tell us something about the inner personalities of all four of these principal characters. Their manner of expressing themselves in language has all the variety of musical counterpoint, in which the changing voices harmonize after strange dissonances. It is notable that the only two of these characters who do not engage in a duet are Mrs. Marwood and Mirabell; perhaps Congreve felt that a scene between a passionate woman and a reluctant man would be too painful for the mood of his comedy. The scene between Fainall and Mrs. Marwood skirts the borders of tragedy, but it ends in reconciliation and an offer of marriage, which ironically can never come to anything in the end if Mirabell is to be successful in forcing a final reunion between Fainall and his wife.

The principal figures in *The Way of the World* are

beautifully characterized by their language, and Congreve has not omitted to pay careful attention to the words of the three servants also. Waitwell is educated enough to be able to express himself in the courtly phrases of Sir Rowland; Foible is fluent enough to play skillfully her role as the chief depositary for the secrets of the main characters. Mincing, Millamant's woman, who is tied into the plot only by being ready to "vouch" with Foible in the last act, is the nonpareil of waiting maids. We feel her youth and her gaiety as she sprinkles her malapropisms among the witty innuendoes of her mistress. Mincing must stand between Mrs. Millamant and Witwoud's wit "like a screen before a great fire," and it is Mincing who gives us the unforgettable picture of Millamant at her toilet, trying to pin up her hair with prose "and all to no purpose. But when your laship pins it up with poetry, it sits so pleasant the next day as anything, and is so pure and so crips." Witwoud interposes, "Indeed, so crips?" and Mincing neatly breaks the butterfly upon a wheel with her retort, "You're such a critic, Mr. Witwoud."

"You're such a critic, Mr. Witwoud"; this remark might fairly be directed against Congreve himself. Perhaps the dramatist unconsciously realized this fact when he put it into the mouth of the incomparable Mincing. Congreve's fools are not fools indeed, and out of the mouths of his servants comes a flow of practical wisdom. Congreve is such a critic that he can rarely resist the temptation to puncture the fabric of society and the self-esteem of his characters who are a part of it. They are none of them people who allow their emotions to dominate them, but they all have emotions which now and then break through the careful guard that is ordinarily put upon them. Congreve's greatest gift was his ability to find words in which different types of human beings could express their true natures amid the intricacies of civilized social intercourse. We moderns, who do not lightly wear our hearts upon our sleeves, may well marvel at his ingenuity and verbal dexterity, perhaps even at his fundamental sanity.

Bibliographical Note on the Text

The first quarto of *The Way of the World* appeared in 1700, the second in 1706. The play was included in the 1710 edition of Congreve's collected works with the text revised and corrected. The chief difference between the two versions is that in the roughly similar quartos there are no scene divisions within the acts; in the collected edition new scenes are indicated, according to the French convention, at the entrance or exit of characters. The present edition is based on the quarto texts but includes many of the revisions and corrections made in the collected edition; the spelling and punctuation have been modernized.

THE PRINCIPAL DATES IN THE LIFE OF WILLIAM CONGREVE

1670   Born at Bardsey, near Leeds, Yorkshire, January 24.

1674-1681   Lived at Youghal and Carrickfergus in Ireland.

1682   Entered Kilkenny School.

1686   Entered Trinity College, Dublin.

1688   The Bloodless Revolution. Accession of William and Mary.

1691   Congreve enrolled for the study of law in the Middle Temple.

1692   Publication of a short novel, *Incognita, or Love and Duty Reconciled*. Poems by Congreve published in Gildon's *Miscellany*. Contributed to Dryden's *Juvenal and Persius*.

1693   *The Old Bachelor* produced in March. *The Double-Dealer* produced in November or December.

1694   Death of Queen Mary. Congreve wrote *The Mourning Muse of Alexis* to commemorate that event.

1695   *Love for Love* produced on April 30 in the new Lincoln's Inn Fields Theatre. Appointed Commissioner for Licensing Hackney Coaches. Essay *Concerning Humour in Comedy*.

1697   *The Mourning Bride,* a tragedy, produced February 27.

1698   Jeremy Collier's *A Short View of the Immorality and Profaneness of the English Stage* published in April. Congreve's *Amendments of Mr. Collier's False and Imperfect Citations* published in July.

1700   *The Way of the World* produced in March. Death of Dryden.

1701   *The Judgment of Paris*, a masque, performed.

1702   Accession of Queen Anne.

1704   Production of *Squire Trelooby*, a farce adapted from Molière's *Monsieur de Pourceaugnac* by Vanbrugh, Congreve, and Walsh.

1705   Appointed Commissioner of Wine Licenses.

1710   First collected edition of Congreve's works, including *Semele*, an opera, published by Jacob Tonson.

1714   Accession of George I. Congreve appointed Secretary to the Island of Jamaica.

1720   Pope dedicated his translation of the *Iliad* to Congreve.

1725   Congreve made his will leaving £200 to Mrs. Anne Bracegirdle and most of his property to Henrietta, Duchess of Marlborough.

1726   Voltaire visited Congreve.

1729   Died in his lodgings at the house of Edward Porter in Surrey Street, Strand, January 19.

THE ARGUMENT OF THE PLAY

[by the editor]

SIR JONATHAN and Lady Wishfort have a daughter Arabella, who marries and becomes the widow of a Mr. Languish. Thereafter she contracts a liaison with Mr. Edward Mirabell, who, fearing that she may become pregnant by him, arranges a marriage between her and Mr. Fainall, a fortune-hunting man about town. Fainall believes that his wife has settled on him the greatest part of her estate. The loveless marriage of the Fainalls is further complicated because Mrs. Fainall continues to be on good terms with Mirabell and because Fainall enters upon a love affair with Mrs. Marwood, who later falls in love with Mirabell. During the course of the play, Mrs. Marwood discovers the old affair between Mirabell and Mrs. Fainall and imparts the news of it to Fainall. Subsequently Mrs. Fainall and Mirabell discover the existence of the affair between Fainall and Mrs. Marwood. Foible, Lady Wishfort's maid, is the only person who, at the beginning of the play, knows of the two extra-marital affairs involved in it.

Lady Wishfort also has a niece, Millamant, a half of whose fortune, £6000, will be forfeited, according to the deceased Sir Jonathan Wishfort's last will and testament, if she does not marry with Lady Wishfort's knowledge and approbation. In that case the £6000 will descend to Mrs. Fainall. Mirabell, who has meanwhile fallen in love with Millamant, pays court to Lady Wishfort in an effort to ingratiate himself with her, but Mrs. Marwood, jealous of Mirabell's attentions to Millamant, reveals to Lady Wishfort his ulterior motives. Lady Wishfort, who herself wishes to wed again, is furious at Mirabell and refuses to allow him to marry Millamant. To secure Lady Wishfort's consent, Mirabell embarks upon a scheme to have his servant, Waitwell, impersonate his uncle, Sir

xviii   THE ARGUMENT OF THE PLAY

Rowland, and pay court to Lady Wishfort. Then, when Lady Wishfort has agreed to marry the supposed Sir Rowland, Mirabell intends to discover the imposture and release her from such an unsuitable engagement, if she will give her consent to his marriage with Millamant. In order that Waitwell may not attempt selfishly to carry through his proposed marriage to Lady Wishfort, Mirabell arranges that his servant shall secretly marry Foible, Lady Wishfort's maid, before undertaking to act the part of Sir Rowland. In the first act of the play Mirabell is waiting for news that the stolen marriage between Waitwell and Foible has taken place.

THE WAY OF THE WORLD

A Comedy

❦

Audire est operæ pretium, procedere recte
Qui mœchis non vultis.—HORAT. Lib. i. Sat. 2.[1]

Metuat doti deprensa.—*Ibid.*[2]

COMMENDATORY VERSES [3]

To Mr. CONGREVE, occasioned by his Comedy called "The
Way of the World."

WHEN pleasure's falling to the low delight,
In the vain joys of the uncertain sight;
No sense of wit when rude spectators know,
But in distorted gesture, farce and show;
How could, great author, your aspiring mind
Dare to write only to the few refined?
Yet though that nice ambition you pursue,
'Tis not in Congreve's power to please but few.
Implicitly devoted to his fame,
Well-dressed barbarians know his awful name;
Though senseless they're of mirth, but when they laugh,

---

[1] It is worth your while to listen, you who do not wish adulterers to succeed in their undertakings.—HORACE, *Satires*, BOOK I, Satire 2, ll. 37-8. [2] Let her fear for the dowry if she is trapped. (apparently referring to Lady Wishfort)—The same, l. 131. [3] *Commendatory Verses* These verses first appeared in the 1710 edition of Congreve's collected works.

1

As they feel wine, but when, till drunk, they quaff.
   On you from fate a lavish portion fell
In every way of writing to excel.
Your muse applause to Arabella[4] brings,
In notes as sweet as Arabella sings.
Whene'er you draw an undissembled woe,
With sweet distress your rural numbers flow;
Pastora's[5] the complaint of every swain,
Pastora still the echo of the plain!
Or if your muse describe, with warming force,
The wounded Frenchman falling from his horse;
And her own William[6] glorious in the strife,
Bestowing on the prostrate foe his life;
You the great act as generously rehearse,
And all the English fury's in your verse.
By your selected scenes and handsome choice,
Ennobled Comedy exalts her voice;[7]
You check unjust esteem and fond desire,
And teach to scorn what else we should admire;
The just impression taught by you we bear,
The player acts the world, the world the player,
Whom still that world unjustly disesteems,
Though he alone professes what he seems.
But when your muse assumes her tragic part,
She conquers and she reigns in every heart;
To mourn with her men cheat their private woe,
And generous pity's all the grief they know.
The widow, who, impatient of delay,
From the town joys must mask it to the play,
Joins with your Mourning Bride's[8] resistless moan,

---

[4] **Arabella** a reference to Congreve's *Ode on Mrs. Arabella Hunt, Singing* [5] **Pastora's** a reference to *The Mourning Muse of Alexis*, in which Congreve laments the death of Queen Mary under the name of Pastora [6] **William** a reference to Congreve's *Pindarique Ode to the King, On his Taking Namur*, in which William III's victory is celebrated [7] **voice** cf. "vocem Comœdia tollit," Horace, *Ars Poetica*, l. 93 [8] **Mourning Bride's** Congreve's tragedy, *The Mourning Bride*, was produced in 1697.

And weeps a loss she slighted, when her own;
You give us torment, and you give us ease,
And vary our afflictions as you please,
Is not a heart so kind as yours in pain,
To load your friends with cares you only feign;
Your friends in grief, composed yourself, to leave?
But 'tis the only way you'll e'er deceive.
Then still, great sir, your moving power employ,
To lull our sorrow, and correct our joy.

R. STEELE[9]

To the Right Honourable

RALPH, EARL OF MONTAGUE,[10] &c.

MY LORD,

Whether the world will arraign me of vanity or not, that I have presumed to dedicate this comedy to your Lordship, I am yet in doubt, though it may be it is some degree of vanity even to doubt of it. One who has at any time had the honour of your Lordship's conversation, cannot be supposed to think very meanly of that which he would prefer[11] to your perusal; yet it were to incur the imputation of too much sufficiency, to pretend to such a merit as might abide the test of your Lordship's censure.

Whatever value may be wanting to this play while yet it is mine, will be sufficiently made up to it when it is once become your Lordship's; and it is my security that I cannot have overrated it more by my dedication than your Lordship will dignify it by your patronage.

That it succeeded on the stage was almost beyond my expectation;[12] for but little of it was prepared for that

[9] R. Steele Sir Richard ("Dick") Steele (1672-1729) [10] Earl of Montague Ralph Montagu (1638?-1709) created Earl of Montagu in 1689 and Duke of Montagu in 1705 [11] prefer offer [12] expectation Actually *The Way of the World* had only a moderate success upon the stage.

general taste which seems now to be predominant in the palates of our audience.

Those characters which are meant to be ridiculed in most of our comedies, are of fools so gross that, in my humble opinion, they should rather disturb than divert the well-natured and reflecting part of an audience; they are rather objects of charity than contempt; and instead of moving our mirth, they ought very often to excite our compassion.

This reflection moved me to design some characters which should appear ridiculous, not so much through a natural folly (which is incorrigible, and therefore not proper for the stage) as through an affected wit; a wit, which, at the same time that it is affected, is also false. As there is some difficulty in the formation of a character of this nature, so there is some hazard which attends the progress of its success upon the stage; for many come to a play so overcharged with criticism that they very often let fly their censure, when through their rashness they have mistaken their aim. This I had occasion lately to observe; for this play had been acted two or three days, before some of these hasty judges could find the leisure to distinguish betwixt the character of a Witwoud and a Truewit.[13]

I must beg your Lordship's pardon for this digression from the true course of this epistle; but that it may not seem altogether impertinent, I beg that I may plead the occasion of it, in part of that excuse of which I stand in need, for recommending this comedy to your protection. It is only by the countenance of your Lordship, and the *few* so qualified, that such who write with care and pains can hope to be distinguished; for the prostituted name of *poet* promiscuously levels all that bear it.

Terence, the most correct writer in the world, had a Scipio and a Lælius,[14] if not to assist him, at least to support him in his reputation; and notwithstanding his

[13] a Witwoud and a Truewit Witwoud in *The Way of the World* and Truewit in Ben Johnson's *Epicœne: or The Silent Woman* (1609) [14] a Scipio and a Lælius Scipio Africanus the Younger and Caius Lælius were friends and patrons of Terence, Roman comic dramatist (B.C. 190?-159?).

extraordinary merit, it may be their countenance was not more than necessary.

The purity of his style, the delicacy of his turns, and the justness of his characters were all of them beauties which the greater part of his audience were incapable of tasting; some of the coarsest strokes of Plautus, so severely censured by Horace, were more likely to affect the multitude, such who come with expectation to laugh at the last act of a play and are better entertained with two or three unseasonable jests than with the artful solution of the *fable*.[15]

As Terence excelled in his performances, so had he great advantages to encourage his undertakings, for he built most on the foundations of Menander;[16] his plots were generally modelled, and his characters ready drawn to his hand. He copied Menander, and Menander had no less light in the formation of his characters from the observations of Theophrastus,[17] of whom he was a disciple; and Theophrastus, it is known, was not only the disciple, but the immediate successor of Aristotle, the first and greatest judge of poetry. These were great models to design by; and the further advantage which Terence possessed, towards giving his plays the due ornaments of purity of style and justness of manners, was not less considerable from the freedom of conversation which was permitted him with Lælius and Scipio, two of the greatest and most polite men of his age. And indeed the privilege of such a conversation is the only certain means of attaining to the perfection of dialogue.

If it has happened in any part of this comedy that I have gained a turn of style or expression more correct, or at least more corrigible,[18] than in those which I have formerly written, I must, with equal pride and gratitude, ascribe it to the honour of your Lordship's admitting me into your conversation, and that of a society where everybody else was so well worthy of you, in your retirement last summer from the town; for it was immediately after, that this comedy was written. If I have failed in my per-

[15] fable plot [16] Menander Greek writer of New Comedy, from whom Terence drew for his plots [17] Theophrastus Greek author of *Ethical Characters* [18] corrigible capable of being corrected

formance, it is only to be regretted, where there were so many not inferior either to a Scipio or a Lælius, that there should be one wanting equal in capacity to a Terence.

If I am not mistaken, poetry is almost the only art which has not yet laid claim to your Lordship's patronage. Architecture and painting, to the great honour of our country, have flourished under your influence and protection. In the meantime, poetry, the eldest sister of all arts, and parent of most, seems to have resigned her birthright, by having neglected to pay her duty to your Lordship, and by permitting others of a later extraction to prepossess that place in your esteem to which none can pretend a better title. Poetry, in its nature, is sacred to the good and great; the relation between them is reciprocal, and they are ever propitious[19] to it. It is the privilege of poetry to address to them, and it is their prerogative alone to give it protection.

This received maxim is a general apology for all writers who consecrate their labours to great men; but I could wish at this time that this address were exempted from the common pretence of all dedications; and that, as I can distinguish your Lordship even among the most deserving, so this offering might become remarkable by some particular instance of respect, which should assure your Lordship that I am, with all due sense of your extreme worthiness and humanity,

MY LORD,
Your Lordship's most obedient and
most obliged humble Servant
WILL. CONGREVE

[19] **propitious** favorably disposed

PROLOGUE

SPOKEN BY MR. BETTERTON[20]

Of those few fools who with ill stars are curst,
Sure scribbling fools, called poets, fare the worst;
For they're a sort of fools which Fortune makes,
And after she has made 'em fools, forsakes.
With Nature's oafs[21] 'tis quite a different case,
For Fortune favours all her[22] idiot-race;
In her own nest the cuckoo-eggs[23] we find,
O'er which she broods to hatch the changeling-kind.
No portion for her own she has to spare,
So much she dotes on her adopted care.

   Poets are bubbles,[24] by the town drawn in,
Suffered at first some trifling stakes to win;
But what unequal hazards do they run!
Each time they write, they venture all they've won;
The squire that's buttered[25] still, is sure to be undone.
This author, heretofore, has found your favour,
But pleads no merit from his past behaviour.
To build on that might prove a vain presumption,
Should grants to poets made admit resumption;
And in Parnassus[26] he must lose his seat,
If it be found a forfeited estate.

   He owns, with toil he wrought the following scenes,
But, if they're naught, ne'er spare him for his pains;
Damn him the more; have no commiseration
For dullness on mature deliberation.

[20] **Mr. Betterton** Thomas Betterton played the part of Fainall in *The Way of the World*. [21] **oafs** children of elves; hence, deformed or stupid children [22] **her** Nature's; in the next line "her own" refers to Fortune. [23] **cuckoo-eggs** The cuckoo was well known for laying its eggs in the nests of other birds for them to hatch. [24] **bubbles** dupes [25] **buttered** loaded with fulsome praise, flattered [26] **Parnassus** a mountain in Greece, sacred to Apollo and the Muses

He swears he'll not resent one hissed-off scene,
Nor, like those peevish wits, his play maintain,
Who, to assert their sense, your taste arraign.[27]
Some plot we think he has, and some new thought;
Some humour too, no farce; but that's a fault.
Satire, he thinks, you ought not to expect;
For so reformed a town who dares correct?
To please, this time, has been his sole pretence;
He'll not instruct, lest it should give offence.
Should he by chance a knave or fool expose,
That hurts none here, sure here are none of those.
In short, our play shall (with your leave to show it)
Give you one instance of a passive poet,
Who to your judgments yields all resignation;
So save or damn, after your own discretion.

[27] arraign denounce

THE WAY OF THE WORLD

✣

Act I

A Chocolate-House

(MIRABELL *and* FAINALL, *rising from cards;* BETTY *waiting*)

MIR. You are a fortunate man, Mr. Fainall.

FAIN. Have we done?

MIR. What you please. I'll play on to entertain you.

FAIN. No, I'll give you your revenge another time, when you are not so indifferent; you are thinking of something else now, and play too negligently. The coldness of a losing gamester lessens the pleasure of the winner. I'd no more play with a man that slighted his ill fortune than I'd make love to a woman who undervalued the loss of her reputation.

MIR. You have a taste extremely delicate and are for refining on your pleasures.

FAIN. Prithee, why so reserved? Something has put you out of humour.

MIR. Not at all. I happen to be grave to-day, and you are gay; that's all.

FAIN. Confess, Millamant and you quarrelled last night, after I left you; my fair cousin has some humours[1] that would tempt the patience of a Stoic.[2] What, some coxcomb came in, and was well received by her, while you were by.

MIR. Witwoud and Petulant, and what was worse, her aunt, your wife's mother, my evil genius; or to sum up all in her own name, my old Lady Wishfort came in.

[1] **humours** states of mind, moods   [2] **Stoic** the school of Stoic philosophy taught that one should be indifferent to pleasure or pain.

11

FAIN. Oh, there it is then! She has a lasting passion for you, and with reason. What, then my wife was there?

MIR. Yes, and Mrs. Marwood, and three or four more, whom I never saw before. Seeing me, they all put on their grave faces, whispered one another; then complained aloud of the vapours,[3] and after fell into a profound silence.

FAIN. They had a mind to be rid of you.

MIR. For which reason I resolved not to stir. At last the good old lady broke through her painful taciturnity with an invective against long visits. I would not have understood her, but Millamant joining in the argument, I rose, and, with a constrained smile, told her, I thought nothing was so easy as to know when a visit began to be troublesome. She reddened, and I withdrew, without expecting[4] her reply.

FAIN. You were to blame to resent what she spoke only in compliance with her aunt.

MIR. She is more mistress of herself than to be under the necessity of such a resignation.

FAIN. What? though half her fortune depends upon her marrying with my lady's approbation?

MIR. I was then in such a humour that I should have been better pleased if she had been less discreet.

FAIN. Now I remember, I wonder not they were weary of you. Last night was one of their cabal-nights;[5] they have 'em three times a week, and meet by turns at one another's apartments, where they come together like the coroner's inquest, to sit upon the murdered reputations of the week. You and I are excluded; and it was once proposed that all the male sex should be excepted.[6] But somebody moved that, to avoid scandal, there might be one man of the community; upon which motion Witwoud and Petulant[7] were enrolled members.

MIR. And who may have been the foundress of this sect? My Lady Wishfort, I warrant, who publishes her detestation of mankind, and full of the vigour of fifty-five, declares

[3] **vapours** melancholy, the blues [4] **expecting** waiting for [5] **cabal-nights** evening parties of a small select society [6] **excepted** left out [7] **Witwoud and Petulant** Together they are equal to one man.

for a friend and ratafia;[8] and let posterity shift for itself, she'll breed no more.

FAIN. The discovery of your sham addresses to her, to conceal your love to her niece, has provoked this separation; had you dissembled better, things might have continued in the state of nature.

MIR. I did as much as man could, with any reasonable conscience; I proceeded to the very last act of flattery with her, and was guilty of a song in her commendation. Nay, I got a friend to put her into a lampoon,[9] and compliment her with the imputation of an affair with a young fellow, which I carried so far that I told her the malicious town took notice that she was grown fat of a sudden; and when she lay in a dropsy,[10] persuaded her she was reported to be in labour. The devil's in't, if an old woman is to be flattered further, unless a man should endeavour downright personally to debauch her; and that my virtue forbade me. But for the discovery of this amour I am indebted to your friend, or your wife's friend, Mrs. Marwood.

FAIN. What should provoke her to be your enemy, unless she has made you advances which you have slighted? Women do not easily forgive omissions of that nature.

MIR. She was always civil to me till of late. I confess I am not one of those coxcombs who are apt to interpret a woman's good manners to her prejudice,[11] and think that she who does not refuse 'em everything can refuse 'em nothing.

FAIN. You are a gallant man, Mirabell; and though you may have cruelty enough not to satisfy a lady's longing, you have too much generosity not to be tender of her honour. Yet you speak with an indifference which seems to be affected, and confesses you are conscious of a negligence.

MIR. You pursue the argument with a distrust that seems to be unaffected, and confesses you are conscious of a concern for which the lady is more indebted to you than is your wife.

[8] ratafia a liqueur flavored with fruit kernels [9] lampoon a personal satire in writing [10] dropsy an abnormal accumulation of fluid in the body [11] prejudice injury, disadvantage

FAIN. Fie, fie, friend! If you grow censorious, I must leave you. I'll look upon the gamesters in the next room.

MIR. Who are they?

FAIN. Petulant and Witwoud. (*To* BETTY) Bring me some chocolate. (*Exit*)

MIR. Betty, what says your clock?

BET. Turned of the last canonical hour,[12] sir. (*Exit*)

MIR. How pertinently the jade answers me! (*Looking on his watch*) Ha? almost one o'clock! O, y'are come!

(*Enter a* SERVANT)

Well, is the grand affair over? You have been something tedious.

SERV. Sir, there's such coupling at Pancras[13] that they stand behind one another, as 'twere in a country dance. Ours was the last couple to lead up,[14] and no hopes appearing of dispatch,[15] besides the parson growing hoarse, we were afraid his lungs would have failed before it came to our turn; so we drove round to Duke's Place,[16] and there they were riveted in a trice.

MIR. So, so, you are sure they are married.

SERV. Married and bedded, sir; I am witness.

MIR. Have you the certificate?

SERV. Here it is, sir.

MIR. Has the tailor brought Waitwell's clothes home, and the new liveries?

SERV. Yes, sir.

MIR. That's well. Do you go home again, d'ye hear, and adjourn the consummation till farther order; bid Waitwell shake his ears, and Dame Partlet[17] rustle up her feath-

---

[12] canonical hour in England, any of the hours from 8 A.M. to 3 P.M., before and after which a marriage cannot legally be performed in a parish church [13] Pancras Pancras Church, where couples could marry without licenses [14] lead up come up [15] dispatch speed [16] Duke's Place In Duke's Place was situated St. James's Church, where also marriages could be performed without licenses. [17] Dame Partlet Pentelote, the hen; Foible is here so called.

ers, and meet me at one o'clock by Rosamond's Pond,[18] that I may see her before she returns to her lady; and as you tender your ears, be secret. (*Exit* SERVANT)

(*Re-enter* FAINALL *and* BETTY)

FAIN. Joy of your success, Mirabell; you look pleased.

MIR. Aye, I have been engaged in a matter of some sort of mirth, which is not yet ripe for discovery. I am glad this is not a cabal-night. I wonder, Fainall, that you who are married, and of consequence should be discreet, will suffer your wife to be of such a party.

FAIN. Faith, I am not jealous. Besides, most who are engaged are women and relations; and for the men, they are of a kind too contemptible to give scandal.

MIR. I am of another opinion. The greater the coxcomb, always the more the scandal; for a woman who is not a fool can have but one reason for associating with a man who is one.

FAIN. Are you jealous as often as you see Witwoud entertained by Millamant?

MIR. Of her understanding I am, if not of her person.

FAIN. You do her wrong; for, to give her her due, she has wit.

MIR. She has beauty enough to make any man think so, and complaisance[19] enough not to contradict him who shall tell her so.

FAIN. For a passionate lover, methinks you are a man somewhat too discerning in the failings of your mistress.

MIR. And for a discerning man, somewhat too passionate a lover; for I like her with all her faults, nay, like her for her faults. Her follies are so natural, or so artful, that they become her; and those affectations which in another woman would be odious, serve but to make her more agreeable. I'll tell thee, Fainall, she once used me with that insolence, that in revenge I took her to pieces, sifted[20] her, and separated her failings; I studied 'em, and got 'em by rote.[21] The

[18] **Rosamond's Pond** a small pond in the southwest corner of St. James's Park   [19] **complaisance** civility   [20] **sifted** examined minutely   [21] **by rote** in a mechanical, routine order

catalogue was so large that I was not without hopes one day or other to hate her heartily: to which end I so used [22] myself to think of 'em that at length, contrary to my design and expectation, they gave me every hour less and less disturbance; till in a few days it became habitual to me to remember 'em without being displeased. They are now grown as familiar to me as my own frailties; and in all probability, in a little time longer I shall like 'em as well.

FAIN. Marry her, marry her! Be half as well acquainted with her charms as you are with her defects, and my life on't, you are your own man again.

MIR. Say you so?

FAIN. Aye, aye, I have experience; I have a wife, and so forth.

(*Enter a* MESSENGER)

MES. Is one Squire Witwoud here?

BET. Yes; what's your business?

MES. I have a letter for him, from his brother Sir Wilfull, which I am charged to deliver into his own hands.

BET. He's in the next room, friend; that way.

(*Exit* MESSENGER)

MIR. What, is the chief of that noble family in town, Sir Wilfull Witwoud?

FAIN. He is expected to-day. Do you know him?

MIR. I have seen him. He promises to be an extraordinary person; I think you have the honour to be related to him.

FAIN. Yes, he is half brother to this Witwoud by a former wife, who was sister to my Lady Wishfort, my wife's mother. If you marry Millamant, you must call cousins too.

MIR. I had rather be his relation than his acquaintance.

FAIN. He comes to town in order to equip himself for travel.

MIR. For travel! Why the man that I mean is above forty.

---

[22] used accustomed

FAIN. No matter for that; 'tis for the honour of England that all Europe should know we have blockheads of all ages.

MIR. I wonder there is not an act of parliament to save the credit of the nation, and prohibit the exportation of fools.

FAIN. By no means; 'tis better as 'tis. 'Tis better to trade with a little loss than to be quite eaten up with being over-stocked.

MIR. Pray, are the follies of this knight-errant[23] and those of the squire his brother anything related?

FAIN. Not at all; Witwoud grows by the knight, like a medlar grafted on a crab.[24] One will melt in your mouth, and t'other set your teeth on edge; one is all pulp, and the other all core.

MIR. So one will be rotten before he be ripe, and the other will be rotten without ever being ripe at all.

FAIN. Sir Wilfull is an odd mixture of bashfulness and obstinacy. But when he's drunk, he's as loving as the monster in *The Tempest*,[25] and much after the same manner. To give t'other[26] his due, he has something of good nature and does not always want wit.

MIR. Not always; but as often as his memory fails him, and his commonplace of comparisons.[27] He is a fool with a good memory and some few scraps of other folks' wit. He is one whose conversation can never be approved, yet it is now and then to be endured. He has indeed one good quality, he is not exceptious;[28] for he so passionately affects the reputation of understanding raillery that he will construe an affront into a jest and call downright rudeness and ill language, satire and fire.

[23] knight-errant wandering or traveling knight   [24] a medlar grafted on a crab A medlar resembles a crab apple; but the former is good to eat when it has begun to decay, the latter is always sour.   [25] the monster in The Tempest Caliban, or Sycorax, his sister, in the adaptation of Shakespeare's play by Dryden and Davenant produced in 1667   [26] t'other Witwoud   [27] commonplace of comparisons memorandum book for noting similarities   [28] exceptious apt to take exceptions, or to object

FAIN. If you have a mind to finish his picture, you have an opportunity to do it at full length. Behold the original!

(*Enter* WITWOUD)

WIT. Afford me your compassion, my dears! Pity me, Fainall! Mirabell, pity me!

MIR. I do from my soul.

FAIN. Why, what's the matter?

WIT. No letters for me, Betty?

BET. Did not a messenger bring you one but now, sir?

WIT. Aye, but no other?

BET. No, sir.

WIT. That's hard, that's very hard. A messenger, a mule, a beast of burden! He has brought me a letter from the fool my brother, as heavy as a panegyric in a funeral sermon, or a copy of commendatory verses from one poet to another. And what's worse, 'tis as sure a forerunner of the author as an epistle dedicatory.

MIR. A fool, and your brother, Witwoud!

WIT. Aye, aye, my half brother. My half brother he is, no nearer upon honour.

MIR. Then 'tis possible he may be but half a fool.

WIT. Good, good, Mirabell, *le drôle!* [29] Good, good; hang him, don't let's talk of him. Fainall, how does your lady? Gad, I say anything in the world to get this fellow out of my head. I beg pardon that I should ask a man of pleasure and the town a question at once so foreign and domestic.[30] But I talk like an old maid at a marriage, I don't know what I say; but she's the best woman in the world.[31]

FAIN. 'Tis well you don't know what you say, or else your commendation would go near to make me either vain or jealous.

WIT. No man in town lives well with a wife but Fainall. Your judgment, Mirabell?

[29] **le drôle!** the facetious (fellow)! [30] **foreign and domestic** foreign to one's interests and domestic in nature, with a reference to foreign and domestic public affairs [31] **the best woman in the world** Witwoud refers to Mrs. Fainall.

Mir. You had better step and ask his wife, if you would be credibly informed.

Wit. Mirabell.

Mir. Aye.

Wit. My dear, I ask ten thousand pardons; gad, I have forgot what I was going to say to you!

Mir. I thank you heartily, heartily.

Wit. No, but prithee excuse me; my memory is such a memory.

Mir. Have a care of such apologies, Witwoud; for I never knew a fool but he affected to complain, either of the spleen[32] or his memory.

Fain. What have you done with Petulant?

Wit. He's reckoning his money, my money it was. I have no luck to-day.

Fain. You may allow him to win of you at play, for you are sure to be too hard for him at repartee; since you monopolize the wit that is between you, the fortune must be his of course.

Mir. I don't find that Petulant confesses the superiority of wit to be your talent, Witwoud.

Wit. Come, come, you are malicious now, and would breed debates. Petulant's my friend, and a very honest fellow, and a very pretty fellow, and has a smattering— faith and troth, a pretty deal of an odd sort of a small wit; nay, I'll do him justice. I'm his friend, I won't wrong him neither. And if he had any judgment in the world, he would not be altogether contemptible. Come, come, don't detract from the merits of my friend.

Fain. You don't take your friend to be over-nicely bred?

Wit. No, no, hang him, the rogue has no manners at all, that I must own. No more breeding than a bum-baily,[33] that I grant you. 'Tis pity, faith; the fellow has fire and life.

Mir. What, courage?

Wit. Hum, faith I don't know as to that; I can't say as

[32] spleen ill-humor coming from a diseased condition of the spleen [33] bum-baily a low order of bailiff, a lesser magistrate

to that. Yes, faith, in a controversy he'll contradict anybody.

MIR. Though 'twere a man whom he feared, or a woman
whom he loved.

WIT. Well, well, he does not always think before he
speaks; we have all our failings. You're too hard upon him,
you are, faith. Let me excuse him. I can defend most of
his faults, except one or two. One he has, that's the truth
on't; if he were my brother, I could not acquit him. That
indeed I could wish were otherwise.

MIR. Aye, marry, what's that, Witwoud?

WIT. Oh, pardon me! Expose the infirmities of my friend?
No, my dear, excuse me there.

FAIN. What, I warrant he's unsincere, or 'tis some such
trifle.

WIT. No, no, what if he be? 'Tis no matter for that; his
wit will excuse that. A wit should no more be sincere than
a woman constant; one argues a decay of parts,[34] as t'other
of beauty.

MIR. Maybe you think him too positive? [35]

WIT. No, no, his being positive is an incentive to argument, and keeps up conversation.

FAIN. Too illiterate?

WIT. That! that's his happiness; his want of learning
gives him the more opportunities to show his natural parts.

MIR. He wants words?

WIT. Aye, but I like him for that now; for his want of
words gives me the pleasure very often to explain his meaning.

FAIN. He's impudent?

WIT. No, that's not it.

MIR. Vain?

WIT. No.

MIR. What! he speaks unseasonable truths sometimes,
because he has not wit enough to invent an evasion?

WIT. Truths! ha! ha! ha! No, no; since you will have it,
I mean he never speaks truth at all, that's all. He will lie

---

[34] parts talent [35] positive dogmatic

like a chambermaid, or a woman of quality's porter. Now that is a fault.

(*Enter a* COACHMAN)

COACH. Is Master Petulant here, mistress?

BET. Yes.

COACH. Three gentlewomen in a coach would speak with him.

FAIN. O brave Petulant! Three!

BET. I'll tell him.

COACH. You must bring two dishes of chocolate and a glass of cinnamon-water.[36]

(*Exeunt* BETTY *and* COACHMAN)

WIT. That should be for two fasting strumpets, and a bawd troubled with wind. [37] Now you may know what the three are.

MIR. You are very free with your friend's acquaintance.

WIT. Aye, aye, friendship without freedom is as dull as love without enjoyment, or wine without toasting. But to tell you a secret, these are trulls[38] whom he allows coach-hire, and something more, by the week, to call on him once a day at public places.

MIR. How!

WIT. You shall see he won't go to 'em, because there's no more company here to take notice of him. Why this is nothing to what he used to do; before he found out this way, I have known him call for himself.

FAIN. Call for himself? What dost thou mean?

WIT. Mean! Why he would slip you out of this chocolate-house, just when you had been talking to him; as soon as your back was turned, whip, he was gone! Then trip to his lodging, clap on a hood and scarf, and a mask, slap into a hackney-coach, and drive hither to the door again in a trice, where he would send in for himself; that I mean, call for himself, wait for himself. Nay, and what's more,

[36] cinnamon-water a mixture of sugar, spirits, powdered cinnamon, and hot water, used as a digestive cordial   [37] wind air generated in the stomach or bowels   [38] trulls trollops, loose women

not finding himself, sometimes leave a letter for himself.

MIR. I confess this is something extraordinary. I believe he waits for himself now, he is so long a-coming. Oh! I ask his pardon.

(*Enter* PETULANT *and* BETTY)

BET. Sir, the coach stays.

PET. Well, well; I come. 'Sbud,[39] a man had as good be a professed midwife as a professed whoremaster, at this rate! To be knocked up and raised at all hours, and in all places! Pox on 'em, I won't come! D'ye hear, tell 'em I won't come. Let 'em snivel and cry their hearts out.

FAIN. You are very cruel, Petulant.

PET. All's one, let it pass. I have a humour to be cruel.

MIR. I hope they are not persons of condition[40] that you use at this rate.

PET. Condition! Condition's a dried fig, if I am not in humour! By this hand, if they were your—a—a—your what-d'ye-call-'ems themselves, they must wait or rub off,[41] if I want appetite.

MIR. What-d'ye-call-'ems! What are they, Witwoud?

WIT. Empresses, my dear; by your what-d'ye-call-'ems he means sultana queens.

PET. Aye, Roxolanas.[42]

MIR. Cry you mercy!

FAIN. Witwoud says they are—

PET. What does he say th'are?

WIT. I? Fine ladies, I say.

PET. Pass on, Witwoud. Harkee,[43] by this light his relations: two co-heiresses his cousins, and an old aunt, who loves caterwauling better than a conventicle.[44]

WIT. Ha! ha! ha! I had a mind to see how the rogue would come off. Ha! ha! ha! Gad, I can't be angry with him, if he had said they were my mother and my sisters.

MIR. No!

[39] 'Sbud a corruption of "God's blood" [40] persons of condition people of high social position [41] rub off make off, clear out [42] Roxolanas Roxolana is the Turkish Sultana in Davenant's *The Siege of Rhodes,* first performed in 1656. [43] Harkee corruption of "Hark ye" [44] conventicle meetinghouse of a noncomformist sect

WIT. No; the rogue's wit and readiness of invention charm me. Dear Petulant!

BET. They are gone, sir, in great anger.

PET. Enough, let 'em trundle.[45] Anger helps complexion, saves paint.

FAIN. This continence is all dissembled; this is in order to have something to brag of the next time he makes court to Millamant, and swear he has abandoned the whole sex for her sake.

MIR. Have you not left off your impudent pretensions there yet? I shall cut your throat some time or other, Petulant, about that business.

PET. Aye, aye, let that pass. There are other throats to be cut.

MIR. Meaning mine, sir?

PET. Not I. I mean nobody; I know nothing. But there are uncles and nephews in the world, and they may be rivals. What then? All's one for that.

MIR. How! harkee Petulant, come hither. Explain, or I shall call your interpreter.[46]

PET. Explain! I know nothing. Why, you have an uncle, have you not, lately come to town, and lodges by my Lady Wishfort's?

MIR. True.

PET. Why, that's enough. You and he are not friends; and if he should marry and have a child, you may be disinherited, ha?

MIR. Where hast thou stumbled upon all this truth?

PET. All's one for that; why, then say I know something.

MIR. Come, thou art an honest fellow, Petulant, and shalt make love to my mistress, thou sha't,[47] faith. What hast thou heard of my uncle?

PET. I? Nothing I. If throats are to be cut, let swords clash! Snug's the word;[48] I shrug and am silent.

MIR. Oh, raillery, raillery! Come, I know thou art in the women's secrets. What, you're a cabalist; I know you

[45] **trundle** roll along [46] **call your interpreter** summon someone or something (a sword?) which will cause you to make an explanation [47] **sha't** shalt [48] **Snug's the word** The watchword is secrecy.

stayed at Millamant's last night, after I went. Was there any mention made of my uncle or me? Tell me. If thou hadst but good nature equal to thy wit, Petulant, Tony Witwoud, who is now thy competitor in fame, would show as dim by thee as a dead whiting's[49] eye by a pearl of orient; he would no more be seen by thee than Mercury is by the sun. Come, I'm sure thou wo't[50] tell me.

PET. If I do, will you grant me common sense then for the future?

MIR. Faith, I'll do what I can for thee, and I'll pray that Heaven may grant it thee in the meantime.

PET. Well, harkee.

(MIRABELL *and* PETULANT *talk apart*)

FAIN. Petulant and you both will find Mirabell as warm a rival as a lover.

WIT. Pshaw! pshaw! That she laughs at Petulant is plain. And for my part, but that it is almost a fashion to admire her, I should—Harkee, to tell you a secret, but let it go no further; between friends, I shall never break my heart for her.

FAIN. How!

WIT. She's handsome; but she's a sort of an uncertain woman.

FAIN. I thought you had died for her.

WIT. Umh—no—

FAIN. She has wit.

WIT. 'Tis what she will hardly allow anybody else. Now, demme,[51] I should hate that, if she were as handsome as Cleopatra. Mirabell is not so sure of her as he thinks for.

FAIN. Why do you think so?

WIT. We stayed pretty late there last night, and heard something of an uncle to Mirabell, who is lately come to town, and is between him and the best part of his estate. Mirabell and he are at some distance, as my Lady Wishfort has been told; and you know she hates Mirabell worse than a Quaker hates a parrot, or than a fishmonger hates

[49] whiting's a fish of the cod family [50] wo't wilt [51] demme damn me

a hard frost. Whether this uncle has seen Mrs. Millamant or not, I cannot say; but there were items of such a treaty being in embryo, and if it should come to life, poor Mirabell would be in some sort unfortunately fobbed,[52] i'faith.

FAIN. 'Tis impossible Millamant should hearken to it.

WIT. Faith, my dear, I can't tell; she's a woman, and a kind of a humourist.[53]

MIR. And this[54] is the sum of what you could collect last night?

PET. The quintessence. Maybe Witwoud knows more; he stayed longer. Besides, they never mind him; they say anything before him.

MIR. I thought you had been the greatest favourite.

PET. Aye, *tête à tête*, but not in public, because I make remarks.

MIR. You do?

PET. Aye, aye, pox, I'm malicious, man! Now he's soft, you know; they are not in awe of him. The fellow's well-bred; he's what you call a what-d'ye-call-'em, a fine gentleman; but he's silly withal.

MIR. I thank you. I know as much as my curiosity requires. Fainall, are you for the Mall?[55]

FAIN. Aye, I'll take a turn before dinner.

WIT. Aye, we'll walk in the Park; the ladies talked of being there.

MIR. I thought you were obliged to watch for your brother Sir Wilfull's arrival.

WIT. No, no, he comes to his aunt's, my Lady Wishfort. Pox on him! I shall be troubled with him too; what shall I do with the fool?

PET. Beg him for his estate, that I may beg you afterwards; and so have but one trouble with you both.

WIT. O rare Petulant! Thou art as quick as fire in a

---

[52] fobbed tricked   [53] humourist a person subject to humours or whims   [54] And this This speech resumes the private conversation between Mirabell and Petulant which has been going on during the dialogue of Fainall and Witwoud.   [55] the Mall a fashionable walk in St. James's Park

frosty morning; thou shalt to the Mall with us, and we'll be very severe.

PET. Enough, I'm in a humour to be severe.

MIR. Are you? Pray then walk by yourselves: let not us be accessory to your putting the ladies out of countenance with your senseless ribaldry, which you roar out aloud as often as they pass by you; and when you have made a handsome woman blush, then you think you have been severe.

PET. What, what? Then let 'em either show their innocence by not understanding what they hear, or else show their discretion by not hearing what they would not be thought to understand.

MIR. But hast not thou then sense enough to know that thou oughtest to be most ashamed thyself, when thou hast put another out of countenance?

PET. Not I, by this hand! I always take blushing either for a sign of guilt or ill breeding.

MIR. I confess you ought to think so. You are in the right, that you may plead the error of your judgment in defence of your practice.

　　　　Where modesty's ill manners, 'tis but fit
　　　　That impudence and malice pass for wit.

　　　　　　　　　　　　　　　　(*Exeunt*)

Act II

St. James's Park

(*Enter* MRS. FAINALL *and* MRS. MARWOOD)

MRS. FAIN. Aye, aye, dear Marwood, if we will be happy, we must find the means in ourselves, and among ourselves. Men are ever in extremes, either doting or averse.[1] While they are lovers, if they have fire and sense, their jealousies are insupportable. And when they cease to

[1] averse reluctant

love, (we ought to think at least) they loath; they look upon us with horror and distaste; they meet us like the ghosts of what we were, and as from such, fly from us.

MRS. MAR. True, 'tis an unhappy circumstance of life that love should ever die before us; and that the man so often should outlive the lover. But say what you will, 'tis better to be left than never to have been loved. To pass our youth in dull indifference, to refuse the sweets of life because they once must leave us, is as preposterous as to wish to have been born old, because we one day must be old. For my part, my youth may wear and waste, but it shall never rust in my possession.

MRS. FAIN. Then it seems you dissemble an aversion to mankind, only in compliance to my mother's humour?

MRS. MAR. Certainly. To be free,[2] I have no taste of those insipid dry discourses with which our sex of force must entertain themselves, apart from men. We may affect endearments to each other, profess eternal friendships, and seem to dote like lovers; but 'tis not in our natures long to persevere. Love will resume his empire in our breasts; and every heart, or soon or late, receive and readmit him as its lawful tyrant.

MRS. FAIN. Bless me, how have I been deceived! Why you profess[3] a libertine!

MRS. MAR. You see my friendship by my freedom.[4] Come, be sincere, acknowledge that your sentiments agree with mine.

MRS. FAIN. Never!

MRS. MAR. You hate mankind?

MRS. FAIN. Heartily, inveterately.

MRS. MAR. Your husband?

MRS. FAIN. Most transcendently; aye, though I say it, meritoriously.

MRS. MAR. Give me your hand upon it.

MRS. FAIN. There.

MRS. MAR. I join with you; what I have said has been to try you.

[2] free frank   [3] profess proclaim yourself   [4] freedom frankness

MRS. FAIN. Is it possible? Dost thou hate those vipers, men?

MRS. MAR. I have done hating 'em, and am now come to despise 'em; the next thing I have to do, is eternally to forget 'em.

MRS. FAIN. There spoke the spirit of an Amazon, a Penthesilea! [5]

MRS. MAR. And yet I am thinking sometimes to carry my aversion further.

MRS. FAIN. How?

MRS. MAR. Faith, by marrying; if I could but find one that loved me very well and would be thoroughly sensible of ill usage, I think I should do myself the violence of undergoing the ceremony.

MRS. FAIN. You would not make him a cuckold? [6]

MRS. MAR. No, but I'd make him believe I did, and that's as bad.

MRS. FAIN. Why had not you as good do it?

MRS. MAR. Oh, if he should ever discover it, he would then know the worst, and be out of his pain; but I would have him ever to continue upon the rack of fear and jealousy.

MRS. FAIN. Ingenious mischief! Would thou wert married to Mirabell.

MRS. MAR. Would I were!

MRS. FAIN. You change colour.

MRS. MAR. Because I hate him.

MRS. FAIN. So do I; but I can hear him named. But what reason have you to hate him in particular?

MRS. MAR. I never loved him; he is, and always was, insufferably proud.

MRS. FAIN. By the reason you give for your aversion, one would think it dissembled; for you have laid a fault to his charge of which his enemies must acquit him.

MRS. MAR. Oh, then it seems you are one of his favour-

[5] Penthesilea Queen of the Amazons, a race or nation of female warriors   [6] cuckold a man whose wife is unfaithful to him

able enemies! Methinks you look a little pale, and now you flush again.

MRS. FAIN. Do I? I think I am a little sick o' the sudden.

MRS. MAR. What ails you?

MRS. FAIN. My husband. Don't you see him? He turned short upon me unawares, and has almost overcome me.

(Enter FAINALL *and* MIRABELL*)*

MRS. MAR. Ha! ha! ha! He comes opportunely for you.

MRS. FAIN. For you, for he has brought Mirabell with him.

FAIN. My dear!

MRS. FAIN. My soul!

FAIN. You don't look well to-day, child.

MRS. FAIN. D'ye think so?

MIR. He is the only man that does, madam.

MRS. FAIN. The only man that would tell me so at least; and the only man from whom I could hear it without mortification.

FAIN. O my dear, I am satisfied of your tenderness; I know you cannot resent anything from me, especially what is an effect of my concern.

MRS. FAIN. Mr. Mirabell, my mother interrupted you in a pleasant relation last night; I would fain hear it out.

MIR. The persons concerned in that affair have yet a tolerable reputation. I am afraid Mr. Fainall will be censorious.[7]

MRS. FAIN. He has a humour more prevailing than his curiosity and will willingly dispense with the hearing of one scandalous story, to avoid giving an occasion to make another by being seen to walk with his wife. This way, Mr. Mirabell, and I dare promise you will oblige us both.

(Exeunt MRS. FAINALL *and* MIRABELL*)*

FAIN. Excellent creature! Well, sure if I should live to be rid of my wife, I should be a miserable man.

MRS. MAR. Aye!

FAIN. For having only that one hope, the accomplish-

---

[7] **censorious** disapprovingly critical

ment of it, of consequence, must put an end to all my hopes; and what a wretch is he who must survive his hopes! Nothing remains when that day comes, but to sit down and weep like Alexander,[8] when he wanted other worlds to conquer.

MRS. MAR. Will you not follow 'em?

FAIN. Faith, I think not.

MRS. MAR. Pray let us; I have a reason.

FAIN. You are not jealous?

MRS. MAR. Of whom?

FAIN. Of Mirabell.

MRS. MAR. If I am, is it inconsistent with my love to you that I am tender of your honour?

FAIN. You would intimate, then, as if there were a fellow-feeling between my wife and him.

MRS. MAR. I think she does not hate him to that degree she would be thought.

FAIN. But he, I fear, is too insensible.

MRS. MAR. It may be you are deceived.

FAIN. It may be so. I do now begin to apprehend it.

MRS. MAR. What?

FAIN. That I have been deceived, madam, and you are false.

MRS. MAR. That I am false! What mean you?

FAIN. To let you know I see through all your little arts. Come, you both[9] love him; and both have equally dissembled your aversion. Your mutual jealousies of one another have made you clash till you have both struck fire. I have seen the warm confession reddening on your cheeks and sparkling from your eyes.

MRS. MAR. You do me wrong.

FAIN. I do not. 'Twas for my ease to oversee[10] and wilfully neglect the gross advances made him by my wife; that by permitting her to be engaged, I might continue unsuspected in my pleasures, and take you oftener to my arms in full security. But could you think, because the

[8] Alexander Alexander the Great, King of Macedon [9] both both Mrs. Marwood and Mrs. Fainall [10] oversee overlook

nodding husband would not wake, that e'er the watchful lover slept?

MRS. MAR. And wherewithal can you reproach me?

FAIN. With infidelity, with loving another, with love of Mirabell.

MRS. MAR. 'Tis false! I challenge you to show an instance that can confirm your groundless accusation. I hate him.

FAIN. And wherefore do you hate him? He is insensible, and your resentment follows his neglect. An instance? The injuries you have done him are a proof, your interposing in his love. What cause had you to make discoveries of his pretended passion? to undeceive the credulous aunt, and be the officious obstacle of his match with Millamant?

MRS. MAR. My obligations to my lady urged me; I had professed a friendship to her, and could not see her easy nature so abused by that dissembler.

FAIN. What, was it conscience then? Professed a friendship! Oh, the pious friendships of the female sex!

MRS. MAR. More tender, more sincere, and more enduring, than all the vain and empty vows of men, whether professing love to us, or mutual faith to one another.

FAIN. Ha! ha! ha! You are my wife's friend too.

MRS. MAR. Shame and ingratitude! Do you reproach me? You, you upbraid me? Have I been false to her, through strict fidelity to you, and sacrificed my friendship to keep my love inviolate? And have you the baseness to charge me with the guilt, unmindful of the merit? To you it should be meritorious, that I have been vicious; and do you reflect that guilt upon me, which should lie buried in your bosom?

FAIN. You misinterpret my reproof. I meant but to remind you of the slight account you once could make of strictest ties, when set in competition with your love to me.

MRS. MAR. 'Tis false; you urged it with deliberate malice! 'Twas spoke in scorn, and I never will forgive it.

FAIN. Your guilt, not your resentment, begets your rage. If yet you loved, you could forgive a jealousy; but you are stung to find you are discovered.

MRS. MAR. It shall be all discovered. You too shall be

discovered; be sure you shall. I can but be exposed. If I do it myself, I shall prevent[11] your baseness.

FAIN. Why, what will you do?

MRS. MAR. Disclose it to your wife; own what has passed between us.

FAIN. Frenzy!

MRS. MAR. By all my wrongs I'll do't! I'll publish to the world the injuries you have done me, both in my fame and fortune! With both I trusted you, you bankrupt in honour, as indigent[12] of wealth.

FAIN. Your fame I have preserved. Your fortune has been bestowed as the prodigality of your love would have it, in pleasures which we both have shared. Yet, had not you been false, I had ere this repaid it. 'Tis true, had you permitted Mirabell with Millamant to have stolen their marriage, my lady had been incensed beyond all means of reconcilement; Millamant had forfeited the moiety[13] of her fortune, which then would have descended to my wife. And wherefore did I marry, but to make lawful prize of a rich widow's wealth, and squander it on love and you?

MRS. MAR. Deceit and frivolous pretence!

FAIN. Death, am I not married? What's pretence? Am I not imprisoned, fettered? Have I not a wife? nay a wife that was a widow, a young widow, a handsome widow; and would be again a widow, but that I have a heart of proof,[14] and something of a constitution to bustle through the ways of wedlock and this world! Will you yet be reconciled to truth and me?

MRS. MAR. Impossible. Truth and you are inconsistent. I hate you, and shall for ever.

FAIN. For loving you?

MRS. MAR. I loathe the name of love after such usage; and next to the guilt with which you would asperse me, I scorn you most. Farewell!

FAIN. Nay, we must not part thus.

[11] prevent anticipate [12] indigent destitute [13] moiety half
[14] proof quality of having been proved or tried

MRS. MAR. Let me go.[15]

FAIN. Come, I'm sorry.

MRS. MAR. I care not, let me go, break my hands, do! I'd leave 'em to get loose.

FAIN. I would not hurt you for the world. Have I no other hold to keep you here?

MRS. MAR. Well, I have deserved it all.

FAIN. You know I love you.

MRS. MAR. Poor dissembling! Oh, that—well, it is not yet—

FAIN. What? what is it not? what is it not yet? It is not yet too late—

MRS. MAR. No, it is not yet too late; I have that comfort.

FAIN. It is, to love another.

MRS. MAR. But not to loathe, detest, abhor mankind, myself, and the whole treacherous world.

FAIN. Nay, this is extravagance. Come, I ask your pardon. No tears. I was to blame; I could not love you and be easy in my doubts. Pray, forbear. I believe you. I'm convinced I've done you wrong; and any way, every way will make amends. I'll hate my wife yet more, damn her! I'll part with her, rob her of all she's worth, and we'll retire somewhere, anywhere, to another world. I'll marry thee; be pacified. 'Sdeath,[16] they come; hide your face, your tears. You have a mask;[17] wear it a moment. This way, this way. Be persuaded.   (*Exeunt*)

(*Re-enter* MIRABELL *and* MRS. FAINALL)

MRS. FAIN. They are here yet.

MIR. They are turning into the other walk.

MRS. FAIN. While I only hated my husband, I could bear to see him; but since I have despised him, he's too offensive.

MIR. Oh, you should hate with prudence.

[15] Let me go. Fainall has evidently seized Mrs. Marwood's hands.   [16] 'Sdeath i.e. God's death   [17] mask At this time masks were worn as substitutes for the modern veil; they were more reputable when used out-of-doors than at a play.

MRS. FAIN. Yes, for I have loved with indiscretion.

MIR. You should have just so much disgust for your husband as may be sufficient to make you relish your lover.

MRS. FAIN. You have been the cause that I have loved without bounds, and would you set limits to that aversion of which you have been the occasion? Why did you make me marry this man?

MIR. Why do we daily commit disagreeable and dangerous actions? To save that idol, reputation. If the familiarities of our loves had produced that consequence[18] of which you were apprehensive, where could you have fixed a father's name with credit, but on a husband? I knew Fainall to be a man lavish of his morals, an interested and professing[19] friend, a false and a designing lover; yet one whose wit and outward fair behaviour have gained a reputation with the town enough to make that woman stand excused who has suffered herself to be won by his addresses. A better man ought not to have been sacrificed to the occasion; a worse had not answered to the purpose. When you are weary of him, you know your remedy.

MRS. FAIN. I ought to stand in some degree of credit with you, Mirabell.

MIR. In justice to you, I have made you privy to my whole design, and put it in your power to ruin or advance my fortune.

MRS. FAIN. Whom have you instructed to represent your pretended uncle?

MIR. Waitwell, my servant.

MRS. FAIN. He is an humble servant to Foible, my mother's woman, and may win her to your interest.

MIR. Care is taken for that. She is won and worn by this time. They were married this morning.

MRS. FAIN. Who?

MIR. Waitwell and Foible. I would not tempt my serv-

---

[18] consequence i.e. a child [19] interested and professing self-interested and making only a pretense (of friendship)

ant to betray me by trusting him too far. If your mother, in hopes to ruin me, should consent to marry my pretended uncle, he might, like Mosca in *The Fox*[20] stand upon terms;[21] so I made him sure beforehand.

MRS. FAIN. So if my poor mother is caught in a contract, you will discover the imposture betimes, and release her by producing a certificate of her gallant's former marriage?

MIR. Yes, upon condition that she consent to my marriage with her niece, and surrender the moiety of her fortune in her possession.[22]

MRS. FAIN. She talked last night of endeavouring at a match between Millamant and your uncle.

MIR. That was by Foible's direction, and my instruction, that she might seem to carry it[23] more privately.

MRS. FAIN. Well, I have an opinion of your success, for I believe my lady will do anything to get a husband; and when she has this, which you have provided for her, I suppose she will submit to anything to get rid of him.

MIR. Yes, I think the good lady would marry anything that resembled a man, though 'twere no more than what a butler could pinch out of a napkin.[24]

MRS. FAIN. Female frailty! We must all come to it, if we live to be old and feel the craving of a false appetite when the true is decayed.

MIR. An old woman's appetite is depraved like that of a girl. 'Tis the green sickness[25] of a second childhood; and, like the faint offer of a latter spring, serves but to usher in the fall, and withers in an affected bloom.

MRS. FAIN. Here's your mistress.

---

[20] **The Fox** Ben Jonson's *Volpone: or The Fox* (1606)   [21] **stand upon terms** insist upon going through with the terms of a contract   [22] **her fortune in her possession** Mrs. Millamant's fortune in Lady Wishfort's possession   [23] **carry it** carry on the business (of marrying Mirabell's pretended uncle)   [24] **What a . . . napkin** referring to a butler's skill in pinching a napkin into a variety of fancy shapes   [25] **green sickness** an anemic disease of young women

(*Enter* Mrs. Millamant, Witwoud, *and* Mincing)

Mir. Here she comes, i'faith, full sail, with her fan spread and her streamers[26] out, and a shoal[27] of fools for tenders.[28] Ha, no, I cry her mercy!

Mrs. Fain. I see but one poor empty sculler;[29] and he tows her woman after him.

Mir. (*To* Mrs. Millamant) You seem to be unattended, madam. You used to have the *beau monde*[30] throng after you, and a flock of gay, fine perukes[31] hovering round you.

Wit. Like moths about a candle. I had like to have lost my comparison for want of breath.

Mrs. Mil. Oh, I have denied myself airs to-day. I have walked as fast through the crowd—

Wit. As a favourite just disgraced, and with as few followers.

Mrs. Mil. Dear Mr. Witwoud, truce with your similitudes;[32] for I'm as sick of 'em—

Wit. As a physician of a good air. I cannot help it, madam, though 'tis against myself.

Mrs. Mil. Yet, again! Mincing, stand between me and his wit.

Wit. Do, Mrs. Mincing, like a screen before a great fire. I confess I do blaze to-day; I am too bright.

Mrs. Fain. But, dear Millamant, why were you so long?

Mrs. Mil. Long! Lord, have I not made violent haste? I have asked every living thing I met for you; I have inquired after you, as after a new fashion.

Wit. Madam, truce with your similitudes. No, you met her husband, and did not ask him for her.

Mrs. Mil. By your leave, Witwoud, that were like in-

[26] streamers flags that float in the wind; cf. Milton's description of Dalila, "Sails filled and streamers waving," *Samson Agonistes* l. 718 [27] shoal school (as of fish), or throng [28] tenders small vessels employed to attend other vessels [29] sculler a boat rowed by one man with two sculls, or short oars; also, the man who uses the sculls. [30] **beau monde** fashionable world [31] **perukes** wigs [32] **similitudes** similes, comparisons

quiring after an old fashion, to ask a husband for his wife.

WIT. Hum, a hit! a hit! a palpable hit![33] I confess it.

MRS. FAIN. You were dressed before I came abroad.

MRS. MIL. Aye, that's true. Oh, but then I had—Mincing, what had I? Why was I so long?

MIN. O mem,[34] your laship[35] stayed to peruse a pecket[36] of letters.

MRS. MIL. Oh, aye, letters; I had letters. I am persecuted with letters. I hate letters. Nobody knows how to write letters, and yet one has 'em, one does not know why. They serve one to pin up one's hair.

WIT. Is that the way? Pray, madam, do you pin up your hair with all your letters? I find I must keep copies.

MRS. MIL. Only with those in verse, Mr. Witwoud. I never pin up my hair with prose. I fancy one's hair would not curl if it were pinned up with prose. I think I tried once, Mincing.

MIN. O mem, I shall never forget it.

MRS. MIL. Aye, poor Mincing tiffed [37] and tiffed all the morning.

MIN. Till I had the cremp[38] in my fingers, I'll vow, mem. And all to no purpose. But when your laship pins it up with poetry, it sits so pleasant the next day as anything, and is so pure and so crips.[39]

WIT. Indeed, so crips?

MIN. You're such a critic, Mr. Witwoud.

MRS. MIL. Mirabell, did you take exceptions last night? Oh, aye, and went away. Now I think on't, I'm angry. No, now I think on't, I'm pleased; for I believe I gave you some pain.

MIR. Does that please you?

MRS. MIL. Infinitely; I love to give pain.

MIR. You would affect a cruelty which is not in your nature; your true vanity is in the power of pleasing.

MRS. MIL. Oh, I ask you pardon for that. One's cruelty is one's power; and when one parts with one's cruelty, one

[33] a palpable hit cf. Osric in *Hamlet,* V, ii, 1. 292   [34] mem contraction for "madam"   [35] laship i.e. ladyship   [36] pecket packet, or package   [37] tiffed dressed the hair   [38] cremp cramp   [39] crips a variation of "crisp" found in some provincial dialects

parts with one's power; and when one has parted with that, I fancy one's old and ugly.

Mir. Aye, aye, suffer your cruelty to ruin the object of your power, to destroy your lover, and then how vain, how lost a thing you'll be! Nay, 'tis true: you are no longer handsome when you've lost your lover; your beauty dies upon the instant. For beauty is the lover's gift; 'tis he bestows your charms, your glass is all a cheat. The ugly and the old, whom the looking-glass mortifies, yet after commendation[40] can be flattered by it, and discover beauties in it; for that reflects our praises, rather than your face.

Mrs. Mil. Oh, the vanity of these men! Fainall, d'ye hear him? If they did not commend us, we were not handsome! Now you must know they could not commend one, if one was not handsome. Beauty the lover's gift! Lord, what is a lover, that it can give? Why, one makes lovers as fast as one pleases, and they live as long as one pleases, and they die as soon as one pleases; and then, if one pleases, one makes more.

Wit. Very pretty. Why, you make no more of making of lovers, madam, than of making so many card-matches.[41]

Mrs. Mil. One no more owes one's beauty to a lover than one's wit to an echo. They can but reflect what we look and say; vain empty things if we are silent or unseen, and want a being.

Mir. Yet to those two vain empty things you owe two the greatest[42] pleasures of your life.

Mrs. Mil. How so?

Mir. To your lover you owe the pleasure of hearing yourselves praised; and to an echo the pleasure of hearing yourselves talk.

Wit. But I know a lady that loves talking so incessantly, she won't give an echo fair play; she has that everlasting rotation of tongue, that an echo must wait till she dies, before it can catch her last words.

[40] after commendation after they have been commended, or praised [41] card-matches pieces of cardboard dipped in melted sulphur and used as matches [42] two the greatest two of the greatest

MRS. MIL. Oh, fiction! Fainall, let us leave these men.

MIR. Draw off Witwoud.   (*Aside to* MRS. FAINALL)

MRS. FAIN. Immediately. I have a word or two for Mr. Witwoud.   (*Exeunt* WITWOUD *and* MRS. FAINALL)

MIR. I would beg a little private audience too. You had the tyranny to deny me last night, though you knew I came to impart a secret to you that concerned my love.

MRS. MIL. You saw I was engaged.

MIR. Unkind! You had the leisure to entertain a herd of fools; things who visit you from their excessive idleness, bestowing on your easiness that time which is the incumbrance of their lives. How can you find delight in such society? It is impossible they should admire you; they are not capable. Or if they were, it should be to you as a mortification, for sure to please a fool is some degree of folly.

MRS. MIL. I please myself. Besides, sometimes to converse with fools is for my health.

MIR. Your health! Is there a worse disease than the conversation of fools?

MRS. MIL. Yes, the vapours; fools are physic[43] for it, next to assafœtida.[44]

MIR. You are not in a course of fools? [45]

MRS. MIL. Mirabell, if you persist in this offensive freedom, you'll displease me. I think I must resolve, after all, not to have you; we shan't agree.

MIR. Not in our physic, it may be.

MRS. MIL. And yet our distemper,[46] in all likelihood, will be the same; for we shall be sick of one another. I shan't endure to be reprimanded nor instructed; 'tis so dull to act always by advice, and so tedious to be told of one's faults—I can't bear it. Well, I won't have you, Mirabell. I'm resolved—I think—you may go. Ha! ha! ha! What would you give that you could help loving me?

MIR. I would give something that you did not know I could not help it.

[43] physic medicine   [44] assafœtida an ill-smelling gum resin, used as a medicine to prevent or alleviate spasms   [45] in a course of fools taking a cure to get rid of fools   [46] distemper disease

MRS. MIL. Come, don't look grave then. Well, what do you say to me?

MIR. I say that a man may as soon make a friend by his wit, or a fortune by his honesty, as win a woman with plain-dealing[47] and sincerity.

MRS. MIL. Sententious Mirabell! Prithee, don't look with that violent and inflexible wise face, like Solomon at the dividing of the child [48] in an old tapestry hanging.

MIR. You are merry, madam, but I would persuade you for one moment to be serious.

MRS. MIL. What, with that face? No, if you keep your countenance, 'tis impossible I should hold mine. Well, after all, there is something very moving in a love-sick face. Ha! ha! ha! Well, I won't laugh; don't be peevish. Heigho! now I'll be melancholy, as melancholy as a watch-light.[49] Well, Mirabell, if ever you will win me, woo me now. Nay, if you are so tedious, fare you well; I see they are walking away.

MIR. Can you not find in the variety of your disposition one moment—

MRS. MIL. To hear you tell me that Foible's married, and your plot like to speed? No.

MIR. But how came you to know it?

MRS. MIL. Without the help of the devil, you can't imagine; unless she should tell me herself. Which of the two it may have been, I will leave you to consider; and when you have done thinking of that, think of me.

(*Exeunt* MRS. MILLAMANT *with* MINCING)

MIR. I have something more—Gone! Think of you? To think of a whirlwind, though 'twere in a whirlwind, were a case of more steady contemplation; a very tranquillity of mind and mansion. A fellow that lives in a windmill has not a more whimsical dwelling than the heart of a man that is lodged in a woman. There is no point of the compass to which they[50] cannot turn, and by which they are

[47] plain-dealing honest, outspoken expression of opinion [48] Solomon . . . child cf. I Kings, III, 16-28 [49] watch-light a slow burning candle for night watches [50] they women

not turned; and by one as well as another, for motion, not method, is their occupation. To know this, and yet continue to be in love, is to be made wise from the dictates of reason, and yet persevere to play the fool by the force of instinct. Oh, here come my pair of turtles! [51] What, billing so sweetly? Is not Valentine's Day over with you yet?

(Enter WAITWELL *and* FOIBLE)

Sirrah, Waitwell, why sure you think you were married for your own recreation, and not for my conveniency.[52]

WAIT. Your pardon, sir. With submission, we have indeed been solacing[53] in lawful delights; but still with an eye to business, sir. I have instructed her as well as I could. If she can take your directions as readily as my instructions, sir, your affairs are in a prosperous way.

MIR. Give you joy, Mrs. Foible.

FOIB. O las,[54] sir, I'm so ashamed! I'm afraid my lady has been in a thousand inquietudes for me. But I protest, sir, I made as much haste as I could.

WAIT. That she did indeed, sir. It was my fault that she did not make more.

MIR. That I believe.

FOIB. But I told my lady as you instructed me, sir, that I had a prospect of seeing Sir Rowland, your uncle; and that I would put her ladyship's picture in my pocket to show him, which I'll be sure to say has made him so enamoured of her beauty, that he burns with impatience to lie at her ladyship's feet and worship the original.

MIR. Excellent Foible! Matrimony has made you eloquent in love.

WAIT. I think she has profited, sir. I think so.

FOIB. You have seen Madam Millamant, sir?

MIR. Yes.

FOIB. I told her, sir, because I did not know that you might find an opportunity; she had so much company last night.

---

[51] **turtles** turtledoves   [52] **conveniency** convenience   [53] **solacing** taking comfort, or pleasure   [54] **O las** Alas

MIR. Your diligence will merit more. In the meantime—
(*Gives money*)

FOIB. O dear sir, your humble servant!

WAIT. Spouse.[55]

MIR. Stand off, sir, not a penny! Go on and prosper, Foible; the lease shall be made good and the farm stocked,[56] if we succeed.

FOIB. I don't question your generosity, sir; and you need not doubt of success. If you have no more commands, sir, I'll be gone; I'm sure my lady is at her toilet and can't dress till I come. Oh, dear, I'm sure that (*looking out*) was Mrs. Marwood that went by in a mask; if she has seen me with you, I'm sure she'll tell my lady. I'll make haste home and prevent her. Your servant, sir. B'w'y,[57] Waitwell. (*Exit*)

WAIT. Sir Rowland, if you please. The jade's so pert upon her preferment[58] she forgets herself.

MIR. Come, sir, will you endeavour to forget yourself, and transform into Sir Rowland?

WAIT. Why, sir, it will be impossible I should remember myself. Married, knighted, and attended [59] all in one day! 'Tis enough to make any man forget himself. The difficulty will be how to recover my acquaintance and familiarity with my former self, and fall from my transformation to a reformation into Waitwell. Nay, I shan't be quite the same Waitwell neither; for, now I remember me, I'm married and can't be my own man again.

Aye, there's my grief; that's the sad change of life,
To lose my title, and yet keep my wife.   (*Exeunt*)

---

[55] Spouse Waitwell evidently tries to take from Foible the money which Mirabell has just given to her.   [56] the lease . . . stocked i.e. I shall be as good as my promise and do even more than that for you.   [57] B'w'y contraction for "God be with you," as is "Good-by"   [58] so . . . preferment so bold because of her advancement (to the state of a married woman)   [59] attended expected, waited for (with a pun upon "waited on")

Act III

A Room in LADY WISHFORT'S *House*

(LADY WISHFORT *at her toilet,* PEG *waiting*)

LADY WISH. Merciful! no news of Foible yet?

PEG. No, madam.

LADY WISH. I have no more patience. If I have not fretted myself till I am pale again, there's no veracity in me! Fetch me the red; the red, do you hear, sweetheart? An arrant ash-colour, as I'm a person! [1] Look you how this wench stirs! Why dost thou not fetch me a little red? Didst thou not hear me, mopus? [2]

PEG. The red ratafia does your ladyship mean, or the cherry-brandy?

LADY WISH. Ratafia, fool! No, fool! Not the ratafia, fool. Grant me patience! I mean the Spanish paper, [3] idiot; complexion, darling. Paint, paint, paint; dost thou understand that, changeling, [4] dangling thy hands like bobbins [5] before thee? Why dost thou not stir, puppet? thou wooden thing upon wires!

PEG. Lord, madam, your ladyship is so impatient! I cannot come at the paint, madam; Mrs. Foible has locked it up and carried the key with her.

LADY WISH. A pox take you both! Fetch me the cherry-brandy then. (*Exit* PEG) I'm as pale and as faint, I look like Mrs. Qualmsick, the curate's wife, that's always breeding. Wench, come, come, wench, what art thou doing? sipping? tasting? Save thee, dost thou not know the bottle?

(*Re-enter* PEG *with a bottle and china cup*)

PEG. Madam, I was looking for a cup.

[1] **a person** a person of distinction; "as I'm a person" is a favorite expression of Lady Wishfort's [2] **mopus** mope, a dull, spiritless person [3] **Spanish paper** a kind of cosmetic [4] **changeling** a child secretly exchanged for another more desirable one in infancy; hence a simpleton or idiot [5] **bobbins** pins or cylinders stuck in a pillow to form a design in making lace

44 WILLIAM CONGREVE

LADY WISH. A cup, save thee! and what a cup hast thou brought! Dost thou take me for a fairy, to drink out of an acorn? Why didst thou not bring thy thimble? Hast thou ne'er a brass thimble clinking in thy pocket with a bit of nutmeg? I warrant thee. Come, fill, fill! So; again. (*One knocks*) See who that is. Set down the bottle first. Here, here, under the table. What, wouldst thou go with the bottle in thy hand, like a tapster? As I'm a person, this wench has lived in an inn upon the road, before she came to me, like Maritornes the Asturian[6] in *Don Quixote!* No Foible yet?

PEG. No, madam; Mrs. Marwood.

LADY WISH. Oh, Marwood; let her come in. Come in, good Marwood.

(*Enter* MRS. MARWOOD)

MRS. MAR. I'm surprised to find your ladyship in dishabillé[7] at this time of day.

LADY WISH. Foible's a lost thing; has been abroad since morning, and never heard of since.

MRS. MAR. I saw her but now, as I came masked through the park, in conference with Mirabell.

LADY WISH. With Mirabell! You call my blood into my face, with mentioning that traitor. She durst not have the confidence! I sent her to negotiate an affair in which, if I'm detected,[8] I'm undone. If that wheedling villain has wrought upon Foible to detect me, I'm ruined. O my dear friend, I'm a wretch of wretches if I'm detected.

MRS. MAR. O madam, you cannot suspect Mrs. Foible's integrity.

LADY WISH. Oh, he carries poison in his tongue that would corrupt integrity itself! If she has given him an opportunity, she has as good as put her integrity into his hands. Ah, dear Marwood, what's integrity to an opportunity? Hark! I hear her! Go, you thing, and send her in. (*Exit* PEG) Dear friend, retire into my closet,[9] that I may examine her with more freedom. You'll pardon me, dear

[6] **Maritornes the Asturian** in Cervantes' *Don Quixote,* Part I. Book III, Chapter ii   [7] **dishabillé** informal clothes   [8] **detected** exposed   [9] **closet** a small room for privacy

friend; I can make bold with you. There are books over
the chimney. Quarles and Prynne,[10] and the *Short View of
the Stage*,[11] with Bunyan's works,[12] to entertain you.

(Extt MRS. MARWOOD)

(Enter FOIBLE)

O Foible, where hast thou been? What hast thou been
doing?

FOIB. Madam, I have seen the party.

LADY WISH. But what hast thou done?

FOIB. Nay, 'tis your ladyship has done, and are to do;
I have only promised. But a man so enamoured, so trans-
ported! Well, here it is,[13] all that is left; all that is not kissed
away. Well, if worshipping of pictures[14] be a sin, poor Sir
Rowland, I say.

LADY WISH. The miniature has been counted like. But
hast thou not betrayed me, Foible? Hast thou not detected
me to that faithless Mirabell? What hadst thou to do with
him in the Park? Answer me, has he got nothing out of thee?

FOIB. *(Aside)* So the devil has been beforehand with
me. What shall I say? *(Aloud)* Alas, madam, could I help
it, if I met that confident thing? Was I in fault? If you had
heard how he used me, and all upon your ladyship's account, I'm sure you would not suspect my fidelity. Nay, if
that had been the worst, I could have borne; but he had
a fling at your ladyship too. And then I could not hold;
but i'faith I gave him his own.

LADY WISH. Me? what did the filthy fellow say?

[10] **Quarles and Prynne** Francis Quarles, a religious poet, author
of *Emblems, Divine and Moral* (1635), and William Prynne,
author of *Histrio-Mastix: The Player's Scourge* (1633), a Puri-
tan attack upon the stage   [11] **the Short View of the Stage**
Jeremy Collier's *A Short View of the Immorality and Profaneness of the English Stage* (1698), which had specifically at-
tacked, among other plays, the earlier comedies of Congreve
[12] **Bunyan's works** In 1692 there had appeared in print one
volume of "The Works of that Eminent Servant of Christ, Mr.
John Bunyan."   [13] **here it is** the picture of Lady Wishfort
which Foible has supposedlv shown to "Sir Rowland"   [14] **worshipping of pictures** the worship of religious pictures in Roman
Catholic churches

Foib. O madam! 'tis a shame to say what he said, with his taunts and his fleers, tossing up his nose. "Humh!" says he. "What, you are a hatching some plot," says he. "You are so early abroad, or catering," says he. "Ferreting for some disbanded [15] officer, I warrant. Half-pay is but thin subsistence," says he. "Well, what pension does your lady propose? Let me see," says he. "What, she must come down pretty deep now, she's superannuated," says he, "and—"

Lady Wish. Ods[16] my life, I'll have him, I'll have him murdered! I'll have him poisoned! Where does he eat? I'll marry a drawer[17] to have him poisoned in his wine! I'll send for Robin from Locket's[18] immediately.

Foib. Poison him? Poisoning's too good for him. Starve him, madam, starve him; marry Sir Rowland, and get him disinherited. Oh, you would bless yourself to hear what he said!

Lady Wish. A villain! "superannuated!"

Foib. "Humh," says he. "I hear you are laying designs against me too," says he, "and Mrs. Millamant is to marry my uncle" (he does not suspect a word of your ladyship); "but," says he, "I'll fit you for that." "I warrant you," says he. "I'll hamper you for that," says he. "You and your old frippery[19] too," says he. "I'll handle you—"

Lady Wish. Audacious villain! "handle" me; would he durst! "Frippery! old frippery!" Was there ever such a foul-mouthed fellow? I'll be married to-morrow; I'll be contracted to-night.

Foib. The sooner the better, madam.

Lady Wish. Will Sir Rowland be here, sayest thou? When, Foible?

Foib. Incontinently,[20] madam. No new sheriff's wife expects the return of her husband after knighthood with that impatience in which Sir Rowland burns for the dear hour of kissing your ladyship's hands after dinner.

---

[15]disbanded discharged   [16]Ods a contraction of "God's"
[17]drawer a drawer of liquor, a waiter   [18]Locket's a fashionable tavern at Charing Cross   [19]frippery castoff clothes   [20]Incontinently immediately

LADY WISH. "Frippery! superannuated! frippery!" I'll frippery the villain; I'll reduce him to frippery and rags! A tatterdemalion![21] I hope to see him hung with tatters, like a Long-Lane penthouse[22] or a gibbet thief. A slandermouthed railer! I warrant the spend-thrift prodigal's in debt as much as the million lottery,[23] or the whole court upon a birthday.[24] I'll spoil his credit with his tailor. Yes, he shall have my niece with her fortune, he shall!

FOIB. He! I hope to see him lodge in Ludgate[25] first, and angle into Blackfriars for brass farthings with an old mitten.

LADY WISH. Aye, dear Foible; thank thee for that, dear Foible. He has put me out of all patience. I shall never recompose my features to receive Sir Rowland with any economy[26] of face. This wretch has fretted me that I am absolutely decayed. Look, Foible.

FOIB. Your ladyship has frowned a little too rashly, indeed, madam. There are some cracks discernible in the white varnish.

LADY WISH. Let me see the glass. "Cracks," sayest thou? Why I am arrantly fleaed;[27] I look like an old peeled wall. Thou must repair me, Foible, before Sir Rowland comes, or I shall never keep up to[28] my picture.

FOIB. I warrant you, madam, a little art once made your picture like you; and now a little of the same art must make you like your picture. Your picture must sit for you, madam.

LADY WISH. But art thou sure Sir Rowland will not fail to come? Or will 'a not fail when he does come? Will he be importunate, Foible, and push? For if he should not be importunate, I shall never break decorums. I shall die with

---

[21] A tatterdemalion a ragged fellow   [22] Long-Lane penthouse a shed attached to a wall or building in Long Lane, noted for the sale of old clothes   [23] the million lottery a government scheme to raise a million pounds by the sale of lottery tickets   [24] a birthday the birthday of a member of the royal family   [25] Ludgate Prison in Blackfriars was used chiefly for debtors; a man at a grated window there solicited money for the prisoners from passers-by in the street.   [26] economy orderly arrangement   [27] fleaed flayed   [28] keep up to look as well as

confusion, if I am forced to advance. Oh no, I can never advance! I shall swoon if he should expect advances. No, I hope Sir Rowland is better bred than to put a lady to the necessity of breaking her forms. I won't be too coy neither. I won't give him despair; but a little disdain is not amiss, a little scorn is alluring.

Fოიჩ. A little scorn becomes your ladyship.

LADY WISH. Yes, but tenderness becomes me best, a sort of dyingness. You see that picture has a sort of a—ha, Foible? a swimmingness in the eyes. Yes, I'll look so. My niece affects it; but she wants features. Is Sir Rowland handsome? Let my toilet be removed. I'll dress above. I'll receive Sir Rowland here. Is he handsome? Don't answer me. I won't know; I'll be surprised, I'll be taken by surprise.

Fოიჩ. By storm, madam. Sir Rowland's a brisk man.

LADY WISH. Is he! Oh, then he'll importune, if he's a brisk man. I shall save decorums if Sir Rowland importunes. I have a mortal terror at the apprehension of offending against decorums. Nothing but importunity can surmount decorums. Oh, I'm glad he's a brisk man. Let my things be removed, good Foible.   (*Exit*)

(*Enter* MRS. FAINALL)

MRS. FAIN. O Foible, I have been in a fright, lest I should come too late! That devil Marwood saw you in the Park with Mirabell, and I'm afraid will discover it to my lady.

Fოიჩ. Discover what, madam?

MRS. FAIN. Nay, nay, put not on that strange face. I am privy to the whole design, and know that Waitwell, to whom thou wert this morning married, is to personate[29] Mirabell's uncle, and as such, winning my lady, to involve her in those difficulties from which Mirabell only must release her, by his making his conditions to have my cousin and her fortune left to her own disposal.

Fოიჩ. O dear madam, I beg your pardon. It was not my confidence in your ladyship that was deficient; but I thought the former good correspondence between your

[29] **personate** impersonate

ladyship and Mr. Mirabell might have hindered his com-
municating this secret.

Mrs. Fain. Dear Foible, forget that.[30]

Foib. O dear madam, Mr. Mirabell is such a sweet,
winning gentleman, but your ladyship is the pattern of
generosity. Sweet lady, to be so good! Mr. Mirabell cannot
choose but be grateful. I find your ladyship has his heart
still. Now, madam, I can safely tell your ladyship our success. Mrs. Marwood had told my lady; but I warrant I
managed myself. I turned it all for the better. I told my
lady that Mr. Mirabell railed at her. I laid horrid things
to his charge, I'll vow; and my lady is so incensed that she'll
be contracted to Sir Rowland to-night, she says. I warrant
I worked her up, that he may have her for asking for, as
they say of a Welsh maidenhead.

Mrs. Fain. O rare Foible!

Foib. I beg your ladyship to acquaint Mr. Mirabell of
his success. I would be seen as little as possible to speak
to him; besides, I believe Madam Marwood watches me.
She has a month's mind;[31] but I know Mr. Mirabell can't
abide her. (Calls) John! Remove my lady's toilet. Madam,
your servant. My lady is so impatient, I fear she'll come
for me if I stay.

Mrs. Fain. I'll go with you up the back stairs, lest I
should meet her.   (Exeunt)

(Re-enter Mrs. Marwood alone)

Mrs. Mar. Indeed, Mrs. Engine,[32] is it thus with you?
Are you become a go-between of this importance? Yes, I
shall watch you. Why this wench is the passe-partout,[33]
a very master-key to everybody's strong-box. My friend
Fainall [34] have you carried it so swimmingly? I thought

[30] forget that Mrs. Fainall seems to give Foible money at this
point.   [31] a month's mind a strong inclination (for Mirabell)
[32] Mrs. Engine i.e. the agent or tool, Foible, whose conversation
with Mrs. Fainall has been overheard by Mrs. Marwood
[33] passe-partout that by which one can pass everywhere   [34] My
friend Fainall Mrs. Fainall, whom Mrs. Marwood is reproaching
for aiding Mirabell in his designs

there was something in it; but it seems it's over with you. Your loathing is not from a want of appetite then, but from a surfeit. Else you could never be so cool to fall from a principal to be an assistant; to procure for him! "A pattern of generosity," that I confess. Well, Mr. Fainall, you have met with your match. O man, man! woman, woman! the devil's an ass; if I were a painter, I would draw him like an idiot, a driveller with a bib and bells. Man should have his head and horns,[35] and woman the rest of him. Poor simple fiend! "Madam Marwood has a month's mind, but he can't abide her." 'Twere better for him you had not been his confessor in that affair, without[36] you could have kept his counsel closer. I shall not prove another pattern of generosity and stalk[37] for him, till he takes his stand to aim at a fortune. He has not obliged me to that with those excesses of himself; and now I'll have none of him. Here comes the good lady, panting ripe; with a heart full of hope, and a head full of care, like any chemist upon the day of projection.[38]

(Re-enter LADY WISHFORT)

LADY WISH. O dear Marwood, what shall I say for this rude forgetfulness? But my dear friend is all goodness.

MRS. MAR. No apologies, dear madam. I have been very well entertained.

LADY WISH. As I'm a person, I am in a very chaos to think I should so forget myself; but I have such an olio[39] of affairs, really I know not what to do. (Calls) Foible! I expect my nephew, Sir Wilfull, every moment too. (Calls) Why, Foible! He means to travel for improvement.

MRS. MAR. Methinks Sir Wilfull should rather think of

[35] horns referring to the horns which were supposed to sprout on the head of a deceived husband, or cuckold   [36] without unless   [37] stalk walk behind something for the purpose of approaching game, here the fortune which Mirabell is going to take his position to aim at   [38] projection the last process of alchemy, in which base metal is transformed into gold or silver by an infusion of the "philosophers' stone"   [39] olio a miscellaneous collection

marrying than travelling at his years. I hear he is turned of forty.

Lady Wish. Oh, he's in less danger of being spoiled by his travels. I am against my nephew's marrying too young. It will be time enough when he comes back and has acquired discretion to choose for himself.

Mrs. Mar Methinks Mrs. Millamant and he would make a very fit match. He may travel afterwards. 'Tis a thing very usual with young gentlemen.

Lady Wish. I promise you I have thought on't; and since 'tis your judgment, I'll think on't again. I assure you I will; I value your judgment extremely. On my word, I'll propose it.

(*Re-enter* Foible)

Come, come, Foible, I had forgot my nephew will be here before dinner. I must make haste.

Foib. Mr. Witwoud and Mr. Petulant are come to dine with your ladyship.

Lady Wish. Oh, dear, I can't appear till I'm dressed. Dear Marwood, shall I be free with you again, and beg you to entertain 'em? I'll make all imaginable haste. Dear friend, excuse me. (*Exeunt* Lady Wishfort *and* Foible)

(*Enter* Mrs. Millamant *and* Mincing)

Mrs. Mil. Sure never anything was so unbred as that odious man! Marwood, your servant.

Mrs. Mar. You have a colour; what's the matter?

Mrs. Mil. That horrid fellow, Petulant, has provoked me into a flame. I have broke my fan. Mincing, lend me yours; is not all the powder out of my hair?

Mrs. Mar. No. What has he done?

Mrs Mil. Nay, he has done nothing; he has only talked. Nay, he has said nothing neither; but he has contradicted everything that has been said. For my part, I thought Witwoud and he would have quarrelled.

Min. I vow, mem, I thought once they would have fit.[40]

Mrs. Mil. Well, 'tis a lamentable thing, I swear, that one

[40] fit fought

has not the liberty of choosing one's acquaintance as one does one's clothes.

MRS. MAR. If we had that liberty, we should be as weary of one set of acquaintance, though never so good, as we are of one suit, though never so fine. A fool and a doily stuff [41] would now and then find days of grace, and be worn for variety.

MRS. MIL. I could consent to wear 'em, if they would wear alike; but fools never wear out, they are such *drap-de-Berry*[42] things! without one could give 'em to one's chambermaid after a day or two.

MRS. MAR. 'Twere better so indeed. Or what think you of the playhouse? A fine, gay, glossy fool should be given there, like a new masking habit, after the masquerade is over, and we have done with the disguise. For a fool's visit is always a disguise, and never admitted by a woman of wit, but to blind [43] her affair with a lover of sense. If you would but appear barefaced now, and own Mirabell, you might as easily put off Petulant and Witwoud as your hood and scarf. And indeed 'tis time, for the town has found it; the secret is grown too big for the pretence. 'Tis like Mrs. Primly's great belly; she may lace it down before, but it burnishes[44] on her hips. Indeed, Millamant, you can no more conceal it than my Lady Strammel can her face, that goodly face, which, in defiance of her Rhenish-wine tea,[45] will not be comprehended [46] in a mask.

MRS. MIL. I'll take my death, Marwood, you are more censorious than a decayed beauty, or a discarded toast.[47] Mincing, tell the men they may come up. My aunt is not dressing here; their folly is less provoking than your malice. (*Exit* MINCING) "The town has found it!" What has it found? That Mirabell loves me is no more a secret than it is a secret that you discovered it to my aunt, or than the reason why you discovered it is a secret.

MRS. MAR. You are nettled.[48]

[41] **doily stuff** a kind of woolen stuff [42] **drap-de-Berry** woolen cloth from the province of Berry in France [43] **blind** conceal [44] **burnishes** shines forth [45] **her Rhenish-wine tea** strong wine instead of tea [46] **comprehended** enclosed [47] **discarded toast** a person whose health used to be drunk [48] **nettled** irritated

Mrs. Mil. You're mistaken. Ridiculous!

Mrs. Mar. Indeed, my dear, you'll tear another fan, if you don't mitigate those violent airs.

Mrs. Mil. O silly! ha! ha! ha! I could laugh immoderately. Poor Mirabell! His constancy to me has quite destroyed his complaisance for all the world beside. I swear, I never enjoined it him to be so coy. If I had the vanity to think he would obey me, I would command him to show more gallantry. 'Tis hardly well-bred to be so particular⁴⁰ on one hand, and so insensible on the other. But I despair to prevail, and so let him follow his own way, ha! ha! ha! Pardon me, dear creature, I must laugh, ha! ha! ha! though I grant you 'tis a little barbarous, ha! ha! ha!

Mrs. Mar. What pity 'tis, so much fine raillery, and delivered with so significant gesture, should be so unhappily directed to miscarry!

Mrs. Mil. Ha? Dear creature, I ask your pardon. I swear I did not mind ⁵⁰ you.

Mrs. Mar. Mr. Mirabell and you both may think it a thing impossible, when I shall tell him by telling you—

Mrs. Mil. Oh, dear, what? For it is the same thing if I hear it, ha! ha! ha!

Mrs. Mar. That I detest him, hate him, madam.

Mrs. Mil. O madam, why so do I. And yet the creature loves me, ha! ha! ha! How can one forbear laughing to think of it! I am a sibyl ⁵¹ if I am not amazed to think what he can see in me. I'll take my death, I think you are handsomer and, within a year or two as young; if you could but stay for me, I should overtake you, but that cannot be. Well, that thought makes me melancholy. Now, I'll be sad.

Mrs. Mar. Your merry note may be changed sooner than you think.

Mrs. Mil. D'ye say so? Then I'm resolved I'll have a song to keep up my spirits.

(*Re-enter* Mincing)

---

⁴⁰ particular specific in his attentions (to Mrs. Millamant)
⁵⁰ mind pay attention to   ⁵¹ sibyl prophetess

Min. The gentlemen stay but to comb,[52] madam, and will wait on you.

Mrs. Mil. Desire Mrs. —, that is in the next room, to sing the song I would have learned yesterday. You shall hear it, madam, not that there's any great matter in it, but 'tis agreeable to my humour.

SONG

(*Set by* Mr. John Eccles *and sung by* Mrs. Hodgson)

I

Love's but the frailty of the mind,
When 'tis not with ambition joined;
A sickly flame, which, if not fed, expires,
And feeding, wastes in self-consuming fires.

II

'Tis not to wound a wanton boy
Or amorous youth, that gives the joy;
But 'tis the glory to have pierced a swain,
For whom inferior beauties sighed in vain.

III

Then I alone the conquest prize,
When I insult a rival's eyes;
If there's delight in love, 'tis when I see
That heart, which others bleed for, bleed for me.

(*Enter* Petulant *and* Witwoud)

Mrs. Mil. Is your animosity composed, gentlemen?

Wit. Raillery, raillery, madam; we have no animosity. We hit off a little wit now and then, but no animosity. The falling-out of wits is like the falling-out of lovers; we agree in the main, like treble and bass. Ha, Petulant?

Pet. Aye, in the main, but when I have a humour to contradict.

Wit. Aye, when he has a humour to contradict, then I contradict too. What, I know my cue. Then we contradict

[52] comb i.e. their wigs

one another like two battledores; for contradictions beget
one another like Jews.

PET. If he says black's black, if I have a humour to say
'tis blue, let that pass; all's one for that. If I have a humour
to prove it, it must be granted.

WIT. Not positively must, but it may, it may.

PET. Yes, it positively must, upon proof positive.

WIT. Aye, upon proof positive it must; but upon proof
presumptive it only may. That's a logical distinction now,
madam.

MRS. MAR. I perceive your debates are of importance
and very learnedly handled.

PET. Importance is one thing, and learning's another; but
a debate's a debate, that I assert.

WIT. Petulant's an enemy to learning; he relies altogether
on his parts.

PET. No, I'm no enemy to learning; it hurts not me.

MRS. MAR. That's a sign indeed it's no enemy to you.

PET. No, no, it's no enemy to anybody but them that
have it.

MRS. MIL. Well, an illiterate man's my aversion; I
wonder at the impudence of any illiterate man to offer to
make love.

WIT. That I confess I wonder at too.

MRS. MIL. Ah! to marry an ignorant that can hardly
read or write!

PET. Why should a man be any further from being married, though he can't read, than he is from being hanged?
The ordinary's[53] paid for setting the psalm, and the parish-
priest for reading the ceremony. And for the rest which is
to follow in both cases, a man may do it without book; so
all's one for that.

MRS. MIL. D'ye hear the creature? Lord, here's company;
I'll be gone.   (*Exeunt* MRS. MILLIMANT *and* MINCING)

(*Enter* SIR WILFULL WITWOUD *in a country riding habit,
and a* SERVANT *to* LADY WISHFORT)

[53] ordinary's clergyman appointed to prepare criminals for the
death penalty.

WIT. In the name of Bartlemew and his fair,[54] what have we here?

MRS. MAR. 'Tis your brother, I fancy. Don't you know him?

WIT. Not I. Yes, I think it is he. I've almost forgot him; I have not seen him since the Revolution.[55]

SERV. (*To* SIR WILFULL) Sir, my lady's dressing. Here's company; if you please to walk in, in the meantime.

SIR WIL. Dressing! What, it's but morning here, I warrant, with you in London; we should count it towards afternoon in our parts, down in Shropshire. Why then, belike, my aunt han't[56] dined yet, ha, friend?

SERV. Your aunt, sir?

SIR WIL. My aunt, sir! Yes, my aunt, sir, and your lady, sir; your lady is my aunt, sir. Why, what, dost thou not know me, friend? Why then send somebody hither that does. How long hast thou lived with thy lady, fellow, ha?

SERV. A week, sir; longer than anybody in the house, except my lady's woman.

SIR WIL. Why then, belike thou dost not know thy lady, if thou seest her, ha, friend?

SERV. Why truly, sir, I cannot safely swear to her face in a morning, before she is dressed. 'Tis like I may give a shrewd guess at her by this time.

SIR WIL. Well, prithee try what thou canst do; if thou canst not guess, inquire her out, dost hear, fellow? And tell her, her nephew, Sir Wilfull Witwoud, is in the house.

SERV. I shall, sir.

SIR WIL. Hold ye, hear me, friend; a word with you in your ear. Prithee who are these gallants?

SERV. Really, sir, I can't tell; here come so many here, 'tis hard to know 'em all.   (*Exit*)

SIR WIL. Oons,[57] this fellow knows less than a starling;[58] I don't think 'a knows his own name.

[54] Bartlemew and his fair Bartholomew Fair, a fair held annually in West Smithfield on St. Bartholomew's Day, August 24 [55] the Revolution the Bloodless, or Glorious, Revolution of 1688 [56] han't hasn't [57] Oons a corruption of "God's wounds" like "Zounds" [58] a starling supposed to be a particularly stupid bird.

MRS. MAR. Mr. Witwoud, your brother is not behind-hand in forgetfulness; I fancy he has forgot you too.

WIT. I hope so. The devil take him that remembers first, I say.

SIR WIL. Save you, gentlemen and lady!

MRS. MAR. For shame, Mr. Witwoud; why don't you speak to him? And you, sir.

WIT. Petulant, speak.

PET. And you, sir.

SIR WIL. No offence, I hope. (*Salutes* MRS. MARWOOD)

MRS. MAR. No sure, sir.

WIT. This is a vile dog; I see that already. No offence! Ha! ha! ha! to him; to him, Petulant, smoke[59] him.

PET. It seems as if you had come a journey, sir; hem, hem.   (*Surveying him round*)

SIR. WIL. Very likely, sir, that it may seem so.

PET. No offence, I hope, sir.

WIT. Smoke the boots, the boots; Petulant, the boots, ha! ha! ha!

SIR WIL. May be not, sir; thereafter[60] as 'tis meant, sir.

PET. Sir, I presume upon the information of your boots.

SIR WIL. Why, 'tis like you may, sir. If you are not satisfied with the information of my boots, sir, if you will step to the stable, you may inquire further of my horse, sir.

PET. Your horse, sir! Your horse is an ass, sir!

SIR WIL. Do you speak by way of offence, sir?

MRS. MAR. The gentleman's merry, that's all sir. (*Aside*) 'Slife,[61] we shall have a quarrel betwixt a horse and an ass, before they find one another out. (*Aloud*) You must not take anything amiss from your friends, sir. You are among your friends here, though it may be you don't know it. If I am not mistaken, you are Sir Wilfull Witwoud.

SIR WIL. Right, lady; I am Sir Wilfull Witwoud, so I write myself; no offence to anybody, I hope; and nephew to the Lady Wishfort of this mansion.

[59] smoke make fun, or game, of [60] thereafter according
[61] 'Slife i.e. God's life

58 **WILLIAM CONGREVE**

MRS. MAR. Don't you know this gentleman, sir?

SIR WIL. Hum! What, sure 'tis not—yea by'r Lady, but 'tis. 'Sheart,[62] I know not whether 'tis or no. Yea, but 'tis, by the Wrekin.[63] Brother Anthony! What Tony, i'faith! What, dost thou not know me? By'r Lady, nor I thee, thou art so becravated and so beperiwigged. 'Sheart, why dost not speak? Art thou o'erjoyed?

WIT. Odso, brother, is it you? Your servant, brother.

SIR WIL. Your servant! Why, yours, sir. Your servant again, 'sheart, and your friend and servant to that, and a— (*puff*) and a flapdragon[64] for your service, sir! and a hare's foot, and a hare's scut[65] for your service, sir, an you be so cold and so courtly!

WIT. No offence, I hope, brother.

SIR WIL. 'Sheart, sir, but there is, and much offence! A pox, is this your Inns o' Court[66] breeding, not to know your friends and your relations, your elders and your betters?

WIT. Why, brother Wilfull of Salop,[67] you may be as short as a Shrewsbury cake, if you please. But I tell you 'tis not modish to know relations in town. You think you're in the country, where great lubberly[68] brothers slabber[69] and kiss one another when they meet, like a call of serjeants.[70] 'Tis not the fashion here; 'tis not indeed, dear brother.

SIR WIL. The fashion's a fool; and you're a fop, dear brother. 'Sheart, I've suspected this. By'r Lady, I conjectured you were a fop, since you began to change the style of your letters, and write in a scrap of paper, gilt round the edges, no broader than a *subpœna*.[71] I might

[62] 'Sheart i.e. God's heart, a favorite oath of Sir Wilfull's [63] the Wrekin a hill in Shropshire [64] flapdragon a raisin snatched from burning brandy and eaten [65] scut short erect tail [66] Inns o' Court the four societies of students and practitioners of the law in England [67] Salop Shropshire, the capital of which is Shrewsbury [68] lubberly clumsy [69] slabber slobber [70] a call of serjeants sergeants-of-law when called, or admitted, to the status of barristers [71] subpœna a writ commanding attendance at a court of law

expect this when you left off, "Honoured brother," and
"hoping you are in good health," and so forth, to begin
with a "Rat me,[72] knight, I'm so sick of a last night's debauch," ods heart, and then tell a familiar tale of a cock
and a bull,[73] and a whore and a bottle, and so conclude.
You could write news before you were out of your time,
when you lived with honest Pumple[74] Nose, the attorney
of Furnival's Inn;[75] you could entreat to be remembered
then to your friends round the Wrekin. We could have gazettes,[76] then, and *Dawks's Letter*,[77] and the *Weekly
Bill*,[78] till of late days.

PET. 'Slife, Witwoud, were you ever an attorney's clerk?
of the family of the Furnivals? Ha! ha! ha!

WIT. Aye, aye, but that was but for a while, not long,
not long. Pshaw! I was not in my own power then; an or-
phan, and this fellow was my guardian. Aye, aye, I was
glad to consent to that man to come to London. He had the
disposal of me then. If I had not agreed to that, I might
have been bound prentice[79] to a felt-maker in Shrewsbury;
this fellow would have bound me to a maker of felts.

SIR WIL. 'Sheart, and better than to be bound to a
maker of fops, where, I suppose, you have served your
time; and now you may set up for yourself.

MRS. MAR. You intend to travel, sir, as I'm informed.

SIR WIL. Belike I may, madam. I may chance to sail
upon the salt seas, if my mind hold.

PET. And the wind serve.

SIR WIL. Serve or not serve, I shan't ask licence of you,
sir; nor the weathercock your companion. I direct my discourse to the lady, sir. 'Tis like my aunt may have told

[72] Rat me a form of cursing, short for "May God rot me," as is
"Drat" [73] a familiar tale of a cock and a bull a well-known
cock-and-bull story, an extravagant tale [74] Pumple i.e. Pimple
[75] Furnival's Inn one of the subordinate inns of court attached
to Lincoln's Inn [76] gazettes news-sheets [77] Dawks's Letter
a news-letter printed from type in imitation of handwriting
[78] the Weekly Bill the official publication of the deaths occurring
in and around London [79] bound prentice bound as an ap-
prentice

you, madam. Yes, I have settled my concerns,[80] I may say now, and am minded to see foreign parts. If an how that the peace[81] holds, whereby, that is, taxes abate.

MRS. MAR. I thought you had designed for France at all adventures.[82]

SIR WIL. I can't tell that; 'tis like I may, and 'tis like I may not. I am somewhat dainty in making a resolution, because when I make it, I keep it. I don't stand shill I, shall I,[83] then; if I say't, I'll do't. But I have thoughts to tarry a small matter in town, to learn somewhat of your lingo[84] first, before I cross the seas. I'd gladly have a spice of your French, as they say, whereby to hold discourse in foreign countries.

MRS. MAR. Here's an academy in town for that use.

SIR WIL. There is? 'Tis like there may.

MRS. MAR. No doubt you will return very much improved.

WIT. Yes, refined, like a Dutch skipper from a whale-fishing.

(Re-enter LADY WISHFORT with FAINALL)

LADY WISH. Nephew, you are welcome.

SIR WIL. Aunt, your servant.

FAIN. Sir Wilfull, your most faithful servant.

SIR WIL. Cousin Fainall, give me your hand.

LADY WISH. Cousin Witwoud, your servant; Mr. Petulant, your servant. Nephew, you are welcome again. Will you drink anything after your journey, nephew, before you eat? Dinner's almost ready.

SIR WIL. I'm very well, I thank you, aunt; however, I thank you for your courteous offer. 'Sheart I was afraid you would have been in the fashion too, and have remembered to have forgot your relations. Here's your cousin Tony; belike I mayn't call him brother for fear of offence.

[80] concerns business affairs [81] the peace the Peace of Ryswick (1697), broken in 1701, the year after *The Way of the World* was first acted [82] at all adventures at all costs [83] Shill I, shall I cf. shilly-shally [84] lingo language, here the French language

Lady Wish. O, he's a rallier,[85] nephew. My cousin's a wit; and your great wits always rally their best friends to choose.[86] When you have been abroad, nephew, you'll understand raillery better. (Fainall and Mrs. Marwood talk apart)

Sir Wil. Why then let him hold his tongue in the meantime, and rail when that day comes.

(Re-enter Mincing)

Min. Mem, I come to acquaint your laship that dinner is impatient.

Sir Wil. Impatient? Why then belike it won't stay till I pull off my boots. Sweetheart, can you help me to a pair of slippers? My man's with his horses, I warrant.

Lady Wish. Fie, fie, nephew, you would not pull off your boots here. Go down into the hall; dinner shall stay for you. My nephew's a little unbred; you'll pardon him, madam. Gentlemen, will you walk? Marwood?

Mrs. Mar. I'll follow you, madam, before Sir Wilfull is ready. (Exeunt all but Mrs. Marwood and Fainall)

Fain. Why then, Foible's a bawd, an errant,[87] rank, match-making bawd. And I, it seems, am a husband, a rank husband; and my wife a very errant, rank wife, all in the way of the world. 'Sdeath, to be a cuckold by anticipation, a cuckold in embryo! Sure I was born with budding antlers, like a young satyr, or a citizen's child.[88] 'Sdeath! to be out-witted, to be out-jilted, out-matrimonied! If I had kept my speed like a stag, 'twere somewhat; but to crawl after, with my horns, like a snail, and be outstripped by my wife, 'tis scurvy wedlock.

Mrs. Mar. Then shake it off. You have often wished for an opportunity to part; and now you have it. But first prevent their plot; the half of Millamant's fortune is too considerable to be parted with, to a foe, to Mirabell.

[85] rallier one who indulges in raillery, or jocose ridicule [86] to choose by choice [87] errant arrant [88] a citizen's child the "citizens" of the business part of London were supposed to be frequently cuckolded by the fine gentlemen of the town

FAIN. Damn him! that had been mine, had you not made that fond [89] discovery. That had been forfeited, had they been married. My wife had added lustre to my horns by that increase of fortune; I could have worn 'em tipped with gold, though my forehead had been furnished like a deputy-lieutenant's hall.

MRS. MAR. They may prove a cap of maintenance[90] to you still, if you can away with[91] your wife. And she's no worse than when you had her. I dare swear she had given up her game before she was married.

FAIN. Hum! that may be. She might throw up her cards; but I'll be hanged if she did not put Pam[92] in her pocket.

MRS. MAR. You married her to keep you; and if you can contrive to have her keep you better than you expected, why should you not keep her longer than you intended?

FAIN. The means, the means.

MRS. MAR. Discover to my lady your wife's conduct; threaten to part with her. My lady loves her, and will come to any composition[93] to save her reputation. Take the opportunity of breaking it, just upon the discovery of this imposture. My lady will be enraged beyond bounds, and sacrifice niece and fortune and all, at that conjuncture. And let me alone to keep her warm; if she should flag in her part, I will not fail to prompt her.

FAIN. Faith, this has an appearance.[94]

MRS. MAR. I'm sorry I hinted to my lady to endeavour a match between Millamant and Sir Wilfull; that may be an obstacle.

FAIN. Oh, for that matter leave me to manage him; I'll

---

[89] fond foolish   [90] a cap of maintenance a term in heraldry for a kind of cap, with two points like horns behind, borne in the arms of certain families; here, the cap is to be used for financial maintenance, or support.   [91] away with endure   [92] Pam the knave of clubs, the highest card in the game of loo. Fainall means that he does not believe, as Mrs. Marwood has just suggested, that his wife completely severed her relations with Mirabell at the time of her marriage.   [93] composition agreement   [94] an appearance a probability, or likelihood (of succeeding)

disable him for that. He will drink like a Dane;[95] after
dinner, I'll set his hand in.

MRS. MAR. Well, how do you stand affected towards
your lady?

FAIN. Why, faith, I'm thinking of it. Let me see. I am
married already, so that's over. My wife has played the
jade with me; well, that's over too. I never loved her, or if
I had, why that would have been over too by this time.
Jealous of her I cannot be, for I am certain;[96] so there's an
end of jealousy. Weary of her I am, and shall be. No,
there's no end of that; no, no, that were too much to hope.
Thus far concerning my repose; now for my reputation. As
to my own, I married not for it, so that's out of the question. And as to my part in my wife's, why she had parted
with hers before; so bringing none to me, she can take
none from me. 'Tis against all rule of play that I should
lose to one who has not wherewithal to stake.

MRS. MAR. Besides, you forget, marriage is honourable.

FAIN. Hum! Faith, and that's well thought on. Marriage
is honourable, as you say; and if so, wherefore should
cuckoldom be a discredit, being derived from so honourable a root?

MRS. MAR. Nay, I know not; if the root be honourable,
why not the branches? [97]

FAIN. So, so; why this point's clear. Well, how do we
proceed?

MRS. MAR. I will contrive a letter which shall be delivered to my lady at the time when that rascal who is to act
Sir Rowland is with her. It shall come as from an unknown
hand, for the less I appear to know of the truth, the better
I can play the incendiary. Besides, I would not have Foible
provoked if I could help it, because you know she knows
some passages. Nay, I expect all will come out; but let the
mine be sprung first, and then I care not if I'm discovered.

FAIN. If the worst come to the worst, I'll turn my wife

[95] drink like a Dane The Danes were notorious for overdrinking.
Cf. *Hamlet* I, iv, ll. 17-22 [96] certain Jealousy is essentially a
suspicion of rivalry, not a certainty of it. [97] the branches i.e. of
the cuckold's horns

to grass.[98] I have already a deed of settlement of the best part of her estate, which I wheedled out of her; and that you shall partake[99] at least.

MRS. MAR. I hope you are convinced that I hate Mirabell now; you'll be no more jealous?

FAIN. Jealous! No, by this kiss. Let husbands be jealous; but let the lover still believe. Or if he doubt, let it be only to endear his pleasure, and prepare the joy that follows, when he proves his mistress true. But let husbands' doubts convert to endless jealousy; or if they have belief, let it corrupt to superstition and blind credulity. I am single, and will herd no more with 'em. True, I wear the badge, but I'll disown the order. And since I take my leave of 'em, I care not if I leave 'em a common motto to their common crest.

> All husbands must or[100] pain or shame endure;
> The wise too jealous are, fools too secure.

(Exeunt)

[98] turn my wife to grass turn her out, as a beast to pasture
[99] partake share   [100] or either

Act IV

[*Scene continues*]

(*Enter* LADY WISHFORT *and* FOIBLE)

LADY WISH. Is Sir Rowland coming, sayest thou, Foible? and are things in order?

FOIB. Yes, madam, I have put wax-lights in the sconces, and placed the footmen in a row in the hall, in their best liveries, with the coachmen and postillion to fill up the equipage.

LADY WISH. Have you pulvilled [1] the coachmen and postillion, that they may not stink of the stable when Sir Rowland comes by?

FOIB. Yes, madam.

LADY WISH. And are the dancers and the music ready.

[1] pulvilled sprinkled with a sweet-scented powder

that he may be entertained in all points with correspondence to his passion?

FOIB. All is ready, madam.

LADY WISH. And—well, and how do I look, Foible?

FOIB. Most killing well, madam.

LADY WISH. Well, and how shall I receive him? In what figure shall I give his heart the first impression? There is a great deal in the first impression. Shall I sit? No, I won't sit, I'll walk; aye, I'll walk from the door upon his entrance; and then turn full upon him. No, that will be too sudden. I'll lie, aye, I'll lie down. I'll receive him in my little dressing-room; there's a couch. Yes, yes, I'll give the first impression on a couch. I won't lie neither, but loll and lean upon one elbow; with one foot a little dangling off, jogging in a thoughtful way. Yes, and then as soon as he appears, start, aye, start and be surprised, and rise to meet him in a pretty disorder. Yes, oh, nothing is more alluring than a levee[2] from a couch, in some confusion; it shows the foot to advantage, and furnishes with blushes and recomposing airs beyond comparison. Hark! there's a coach.

FOIB. 'Tis he, madam.

LADY WISH. Oh dear, has my nephew made his addresses to Millamant? I ordered him.

FOIB. Sir Wilfull is set in to drinking, madam, in the parlour.

LADY WISH. Ods my life, I'll send him to her. Call her down, Foible; bring her hither. I'll send him as I go. When they are together, then come to me, Foible, that I may not be too long alone with Sir Rowland.   (*Exit*)

(*Enter* MRS. MILLAMANT *and* MRS. FAINALL)

FOIB. Madam, I stayed here, to tell your ladyship that Mr. Mirabell has waited this half hour for an opportunity to talk with you, though my lady's orders were to leave you and Sir Wilfull together. Shall I tell Mr. Mirabell that you are at leisure?

MRS. MIL. No, what would the dear man have? I am thoughtful, and would amuse myself; bid him come another time.

[2] levee the act of rising

"There never yet was woman made,[3]
  Nor shall, but to be cursed."

(Repeating and walking about)

That's hard!

MRS. FAIN. You are very fond of Sir John Suckling to-day, Millamant, and the poets.

MRS. MIL. He? Aye, and filthy verses; so I am.

FOIB. Sir Wilfull is coming, madam. Shall I send Mr. Mirabell away?

MRS. MIL. Aye, if you please, Foible, send him away, or send him hither; just as you will, dear Foible. I think I'll see him; shall I? Aye, let the wretch come. *(Exit* FOIBLE*)*
  "Thyrsis, a youth of the inspired train." [4]

(Repeating)

Dear Fainall, entertain Sir Wilfull. Thou hast philosophy to undergo[5] a fool; thou art married and hast patience. I would confer with my own thoughts.

MRS. FAIN. I am obliged to you, that you would make me your proxy in this affair; but I have business of my own.

(Enter SIR WILFULL*)*

O Sir Wilfull, you are come at the critical instant. There's your mistress up to the ears in love and contemplation; pursue your point, now or never.

SIR WIL. Yes; my aunt will have it so. I would gladly have been encouraged with a bottle or two, because I'm somewhat wary at first, before I am acquainted. *(This while* MILLAMANT *walks about repeating to herself)* But I hope, after a time, I shall break my mind; that is, upon

[3] There never yet was woman made a quotation from a lyric poem by Sir John Suckling (1609-1642), which begins with these lines [4] Thyrsis, a youth of the inspired train a quotation from *The Story of Phœbus and Daphne, Applied,* a poem by Edmund Waller (1606-1687), which begins as follows:

> Thyrsis, a youth of the inspired train,
> Fair Sacharissa loved, but loved in vain.
> Like Phœbus sung the no less amorous boy;
> Like Daphne she, as lovely, and as coy!

[5] undergo endure

further acquaintance. So for the present, cousin, I'll take my leave. If so be you'll be so kind to make my excuse, I'll return to my company.

Mrs. Fain. Oh, fie, Sir Wilfull! What, you must not be daunted.

Sir Wil. Daunted! No, that's not it. It is not so much for that; for if so be that I set on't, I'll do't. But only for the present; 'tis sufficient till further acquaintance, that's all. Your servant.

Mrs. Fain. Nay, I'll swear you shall never lose so favourable an opportunity, if I can help it. I'll leave you together and lock the door.   (*Exit*)

Sir Wil. Nay, nay, cousin. I have forgot my gloves. What d'ye do? 'Sheart, 'a[6] has locked the door indeed, I think. Nay, Cousin Fainall, open the door! Pshaw, what a vixen trick is this? Nay, now 'a has seen me too. Cousin, I made bold to pass through as it were. I think this door's enchanted!

Mrs. Mil. (*Repeating*)

> "I prithee spare me, gentle boy,[7]
> Press me no more for that slight toy—"

Sir Wil. Anan?[8] Cousin, your servant.
Mrs. Mil. (*Repeating*)

> "That foolish trifle of a heart—"

Sir Wilfull!

Sir Wil. Yes. Your servant. No offence, I hope, cousin.
Mrs. Mil. (*Repeating*)

> "I swear it will not do its part,
> Though thou dost thine, employ'st thy power and art."

Natural, easy Suckling!

Sir Wil. Anan? Suckling? No such suckling neither, cousin, nor stripling; I thank Heaven, I'm no minor.

[6] 'a for "she" (more usually for "he")   [7] I prithee spare me, gentle boy A "Song" by Suckling begins with these lines, followed by those that Millamant quotes in her next two speeches.
[8] Anan? an expression equivalent to "What did you say?"

MRS. MIL. Ah, rustic! ruder than Gothic! [9]

SIR WIL. Well, well, I shall understand your lingo one of these days, cousin; in the meanwhile I must answer in plain English.

MRS. MIL. Have you any business with me, Sir Wilfull?

SIR WIL. Not at present, cousin. Yes, I made bold to see, to come and know if that how you were disposed to fetch a walk this evening; if so be that I might not be troublesome, I would have fought [10] a walk with you.

MRS. MIL. A walk! What then?

SIR WIL. Nay, nothing. Only for the walk's sake, that's all.

MRS. MIL. I nauseate walking; 'tis a country diversion. I loathe the country and everything that relates to it.

SIR WIL. Indeed! hah! Look ye, look ye, you do? Nay, 'tis like you may. Here are choice of pastimes here in town, as plays and the like; that must be confessed indeed.

MRS. MIL. *Ah, l'étourdi!* [11] I hate the town too.

SIR WIL. Dear heart, that's much. Hah! that you should hate 'em both! Hah! 'tis like you may; there are some can't relish the town, and others can't away with the country. 'Tis like you may be one of those, cousin.

MRS. MIL. Ha! ha! ha! Yes, 'tis like I may. You have nothing further to say to me?

SIR WIL. Not at present, cousin. 'Tis like when I have an opportunity to be more private, I may break my mind in some measure. I conjecture you partly guess—however, that's as time shall try; but spare to speak and spare to speed, [12] as they say.

MRS. MIL. If it is of no great importance, Sir Wilfull, you will oblige me to leave me; I have just now a little business—

SIR WIL. Enough, enough, cousin, yes, yes, all a case; [13] when you're disposed, when you're disposed. Now's as well as another time; and another time as well as now. All's one for that. Yes, yes, if your concerns call you, there's no

---

[9] **Gothic** Goths, a barbarous Teutonic tribe.   [10] fought a provincial form of "fetched"   [11] Ah l'étourdi! Oh, the stupid (fellow)!   [12] spare to speak and spare to speed a proverb meaning "If you don't talk, you won't succeed"   [13] all a case all the same

haste; it will keep cold, as they say. Cousin, your servant.
I think this door's locked.

MRS. MIL. You may go this way, sir.

SIR WIL. Your servant; then with your leave I'll return
to my company.

MRS. MIL. Aye, aye; ha! ha! ha!

"Like Phœbus sung the no less amorous boy."

(*Enter* MIRABELL)

MIR. "Like Daphne she, as lovely and as coy."
Do you lock yourself up from me, to make my search more
curious? [14] Or is this pretty artifice contrived, to signify
that here the chase must end and my pursuit be crowned,
for you can fly no further?

MRS. MIL. Vanity! No. I'll fly and be followed to the last
moment. Though I am upon the very verge of matrimony,
I expect you should solicit me as much as if I were waver-
ing at the grate of a monastery, with one foot over the
threshold. I'll be solicited to the very last, nay and afterwards.

MIR. What, after the last?

MRS. MIL. Oh, I should think I was poor and had nothing to bestow, if I were reduced to an inglorious ease and
freed from the agreeable fatigues of solicitation.

MIR. But do not you know that when favours are con-
ferred upon instant [15] and tedious solicitation, that they
diminish in their value, and that both the giver loses the
grace, and the receiver lessens his pleasure?

MRS. MIL. It may be in things of common application;
but never sure in love. Oh, I hate a lover that can dare to
think he draws a moment's air independent on the bounty
of his mistress. There is not so impudent a thing in nature
as the saucy look of an assured man, confident of success.
The pedantic arrogance of a very husband has not so pragmatical [16] an air. Ah! I'll never marry, unless I am first
made sure of my will and pleasure.

MIR. Would you have 'em both before marriage? Or will

[14] **curious** painstaking, difficult   [15] **instant** pressing, urgent
[16] **pragmatical** matter-of-fact, businesslike

you be contented with the first now, and stay for the other till after grace?

MRS. MIL. Ah! don't be impertinent.[17] My dear liberty, shall I leave thee? My faithful solitude, my darling contemplation, must I bid you then adieu? Ay-h adieu, my morning thoughts, agreeable wakings, indolent slumbers, all ye *douceurs*,[18] ye *sommeils du matin*,[19] adieu. I can't do't, 'tis more than impossible. Positively, Mirabell, I'll lie abed in a morning as long as I please.

MIR. Then I'll get up in a morning as early as I please.

MRS. MIL. Ah! idle creature, get up when you will. And d'ye hear, I won't be called names after I'm married; positively I won't be called names.

MIR. Names!

MRS. MIL. Aye, as wife, spouse, my dear, joy, jewel, love, sweetheart, and the rest of that nauseous cant, in which men and their wives are so fulsomely familiar; I shall never bear that. Good Mirabell, don't let us be familiar or fond, nor kiss before folks, like my Lady Fadler[20] and Sir Francis; nor go to Hyde Park together the first Sunday in a new chariot, to provoke eyes and whispers, and then never be seen there together again, as if we were proud of one another the first week, and ashamed of one another ever after. Let us never visit together, nor go to a play together. But let us be very strange and well-bred; let us be as strange as if we had been married a great while, and as well-bred as if we were not married at all.

MIR. Have you any more conditions to offer? Hitherto your demands are pretty reasonable.

MRS. MIL. Trifles! As liberty to pay and receive visits to and from whom I please; to write and receive letters, without interrogatories[21] or wry faces on your part; to wear what I please, and choose conversation with regard only to my own taste; to have no obligation upon me to converse with wits that I don't like, because they are your acquaint-

[17] impertinent not restrained within the bounds of propriety   [18] douceurs sweetnesses, pleasures   [19] sommeils du matin morning sleeps   [20] Lady Fadler To faddle is to fondle, or fuss. cf. fiddle-faddle   [21] interrogatories questionings

THE WAY OF THE WORLD

ance, or to be intimate with fools, because they may be your relations. Come to dinner when I please; dine in my dressing-room when I'm out of humour, without giving a reason. To have my closet inviolate; to be sole empress of my tea-table, which you must never presume to approach without first asking leave. And lastly, wherever I am, you shall always knock at the door before you come in. These articles subscribed, if I continue to endure you a little longer, I may by degrees dwindle into a wife.

Mɪʀ. Your bill of fare is something advanced in this latter account. Well, have I liberty to offer conditions, that when you are dwindled into a wife, I may not be beyond measure enlarged into a husband?

Mʀs. Mɪʟ. You have free leave. Propose your utmost; speak and spare not.

Mɪʀ. I thank you. *Imprimis*[22] then, I covenant[23] that your acquaintance be general; that you admit no sworn confidante, or intimate of your own sex; no she friend to screen her affairs under your countenance, and tempt you to make trial of a mutual secrecy. No decoy-duck to wheedle you[24] a fop, scrambling[25] to the play in a mask; then bring you home in a pretended fright, when you think you shall be found out, and rail at me for missing the play, and disappointing the frolic which you had to pick me up and prove my constancy.

Mʀs. Mɪʟ. Detestable *imprimis!* I go to the play in a mask!

Mɪʀ. *Item,* I article that you continue to like your own face, as long as I shall; and while it passes current with me, that you endeavour not to new-coin it. To which end, together with all vizards for the day, I prohibit all masks for the night, made of oiled-skins and I know not what: hog's bones, hare's gall, pig-water,[26] and the marrow of a roasted cat. In short, I forbid all commerce with the gen-

[22] Imprimis in the first place [23] covenant make as the condition of a formal agreement [24] wheedle you obtain for you by cajolery [25] scrambling struggling unceremoniously [26] pig-water The urine of pigs was used as an ingredient in cosmetics

tlewoman in What-d'ye-call-it Court. *Item*, I shut my doors
against all bawds with baskets, and pennyworths of mus-
lin, china, fans, atlases,[27] etc. *Item*, when you shall be
breeding—

Mrs. Mil. Ah! name it not.

Mir. Which may be presumed, with a blessing on our
endeavours—

Mrs. Mil. Odious endeavours!

Mir. I denounce against all strait-lacing, squeezing for
a shape, till you mould my boy's head like a sugar-loaf,
and instead of a man child, make me father to a crooked
billet.[28] Lastly, to the dominion of the tea-table I submit,
but with *proviso*[29] that you exceed not in your province,
but restrain yourself to native and simple tea-table drinks,
as tea, chocolate, and coffee, as likewise to genuine and
authorized tea-table talk, such as mending fashions, spoil-
ing reputations, railing at absent friends, and so forth; but
that on no account you encroach upon the men's prerogative, and presume to drink healths, or toast fellows; for
prevention of which, I banish all foreign forces, all auxil-
iaries to the tea-table, as orange-brandy, all aniseed, cinnamon, citron, and Barbadoes waters,[30] together with ratafia
and the most noble spirit of clary.[31] But for cowslip-wine,
poppy-water, and all dormitives,[32] those I allow. These
provisos admitted, in other things I may prove a tractable
and complying husband.

Mrs. Mil. O horrid *provisos!* filthy strong-waters! I toast
fellows, odious men! I hate your odious *provisos*.

Mir. Then we're agreed. Shall I kiss your hand upon the
contract? And here comes one to be a witness to the seal-
ing of the deed.

(*Re-enter* Mrs. Fainall)

---

[27] atlases atlas was a rich kind of satin made in the Orient.
[28] billet a small stick [29] proviso conditional stipulation This
scene is often known as "the *proviso* scene." [30] Barbadoes
waters brandy or cordial flavored with orange and lemon peel
[31] clary clary water, a composition of clary flowers with brandy
and various spices [32] dormitives drinks to promote sleep

Mrs. Mil. Fainall, what shall I do? Shall I have him? I think I must have him.

Mrs. Fain. Aye, aye, take him, take him; what should you do?

Mrs. Mil. Well then—I'll take my death I'm in a horrid fright. Fainall, I shall never say it. Well—I think—I'll endure you.

Mrs. Fain. Fie! fie! have him, have him, and tell him so in plain terms; for I am sure you have a mind to him.

Mrs. Mil. Are you? I think I have; and the horrid man looks as if he thought so too. Well, you ridiculous thing you, I'll have you; I won't be kissed, nor I won't be thanked. Here, kiss my hand though. So, hold your tongue now, and don't say a word.

Mrs. Fain. Mirabell, there's a necessity for your obedience; you have neither time to talk nor stay. My mother is coming; and in my conscience, if she should see you, would fall into fits and maybe not recover, time enough to return to Sir Rowland, who, as Foible tells me, is in a fair way to succeed. Therefore spare your ecstacies for another occasion, and slip down the back-stairs, where Foible waits to consult you.

Mrs. Mil. Aye, go, go. In the meantime I suppose you have said something to please me.

Mir. I am all obedience.   (*Exit*)

Mrs. Fain. Yonder Sir Wilfull's drunk, and so noisy that my mother has been forced to leave Sir Rowland to appease him; but he answers her only with singing and drinking. What they may have done by this time I know not; but Petulant and he were upon quarrelling as I came by.

Mrs. Mil. Well, if Mirabell should not make a good husband, I am a lost thing; for I find I love him violently.

Mrs. Fain. So it seems; for you mind not what's said to you. If you doubt him, you had best take up with Sir Wilfull.

Mrs. Mil. How can you name that superannuated lubber? [33] foh!

[33] superannuated lubber old, clumsy fellow

74   WILLIAM CONGREVE

(Enter WITWOUD, *from drinking)*

MRS. FAIN. So, is the fray made up, that you have left 'em?

WIT. Left 'em? I could stay no longer. I have laughed like ten christenings; I am tipsy with laughing. If I had stayed any longer I should have burst; I must have been let out and pieced in the sides like an unsized camlet.[34] Yes, yes, the fray is composed; my lady came in like a *noli prosequi*[35] and stopped the proceedings.

MRS. MIL. What was the dispute?

WIT. That's the jest; there was no dispute. They could neither of 'em speak for rage, and so fell a-sputtering at one another like two roasting apples.

(Enter PETULANT, *drunk)*

Now, Petulant? All's over, all's well? Gad, my head begins to whim it[36] about. Why dost thou not speak? Thou art both as drunk and as mute as a fish.

PET. Look you, Mrs. Millamant, if you can love me, dear nymph, say it, and that's the conclusion. Pass on, or pass off; that's all.

WIT. Thou hast uttered volumes, folios, in less than *decimo sexto*,[37] my dear Lacedemonian.[38] Sirrah, Petulant, thou art an epitomizer[39] of words.

PET. Witwoud, you are an annihilator of sense.

WIT. Thou art a retailer of phrases and dost deal in remnants of remnants, like a maker of pincushions; thou art in truth (metaphorically speaking) a speaker of shorthand.[40]

PET. Thou art (without a figure) just one half of an ass,

[34] unsized camlet a garment made of unsized, i.e. unstiffened, camlet, a costly fabric of satin weave made in Asia [35] noli prosequi *nolle prosequi,* an entry on a record indicating that there will be no further prosecution of a law suit [36] whim it spin [37] decimo sexto a book consisting of sheets, each of which is folded into sixteen leaves; hence, a small-sized book compared with a folio, in which each of the sheets is folded into two leaves [38] Lacedemonian Spartan, a cant name for a good fellow [39] epitomizer summarizer [40] shorthand early stenography

and Baldwin[41] yonder, thy half brother, is the rest. A Gemini[42] of asses split would make just four of you.

WIT. Thou dost bite, my dear mustard-seed; kiss me for that.

PET. Stand off! I'll kiss no more males. I have kissed your twin yonder in a humour of reconciliation, till he (*hiccup*) rises upon my stomach like a radish.

MRS. MIL. Eh! filthy creature! What was the quarrel?

PET. There was no quarrel; there might have been a quarrel.

WIT. If there had been words enow[43] between 'em to have expressed provocation, they had gone together by the ears like a pair of castanets.

PET. You were the quarrel.

MRS. MIL. Me!

PET. If I have a humour to quarrel, I can make less matters conclude premises. If you are not handsome, what then, if I have a humour to prove it? If I shall have my reward, say so; if not, fight for your face the next time yourself. I'll go sleep.

WIT. Do, wrap thyself up like a wood-louse, and dream revenge; and hear me, if thou canst learn to write by tomorrow morning, pen me a challenge. I'll carry it for thee.

PET. Carry your mistress's monkey a spider! Go flea dogs, and read romances! I'll go to bed to my maid.

(*Exit*)

MRS. FAIN. He's horridly drunk. How came you all in this pickle?

WIT. A plot! a plot! to get rid of the knight. Your husband's advice; but he sneaked off.

(*Re-enter* SIR WILFUL *drunk, and* LADY WISHFORT)

LADY WISH. Out upon't, out upon't! At years of discretion, and comport yourself at this rantipole[44] rate!

SIR WIL. No offence, aunt.

[41] Baldwin a name given to the ass in the story of Reynard the Fox [42] A Gemini a pair of twins (Castor and Pollux in the third sign of the zodiac) [43] enow enough [44] rantipole wild, rakish

LADY WISH. Offence? As I'm a person, I'm ashamed of you. Fogh! how you stink of wine! D'ye think my niece will ever endure such a borachio![45] you're an absolute borachio.

SIR WIL. Borachio!

LADY WISH. At a time when you should commence an amour, and put your best foot foremost—

SIR WIL. 'Sheart, an you grutch[46] me your liquor, make a bill. Give me more drink, and take my purse.

(Sings)   "Prithee fill me the glass,
              Till it laugh in my face,
          With ale that is potent and mellow;
              He that whines for a lass
              Is an ignorant ass,
          For a bumper[47] has not its fellow."

But if you would have me marry my cousin, say the word, and I'll do't. Wilfull will do't; that's the word. Wilfull will do't; that's my crest. My motto I have forgot.

LADY WISH. My nephew's a little overtaken,[48] cousin, but 'tis with drinking your health. O' my word you are obliged to him.

SIR WIL. In vino veritas,[49] aunt. If I drunk your health to-day, cousin, I am a borachio. But if you have a mind to be married, say the word, and send for the piper; Wilfull will do't. If not, dust it away, and let's have t'other round. Tony! Ods-heart, where's Tony? Tony's an honest fellow; but he spits after a bumper, and that's a fault.

(Sings)   "We'll drink, and we'll never ha' done, boys,
              Put the glass then around with the sun, boys;
          Let Apollo's example invite us;
              For he's drunk every night,

---

[45] borachio a large leather bottle to hold wine; hence, a drunkard cf. Borachio in *Much Ado About Nothing* (III, iii, ll. 110-112) [46] grutch grudge [47] bumper a cap or glass filled to the brim [48] overtaken overcome, intoxicated [49] In vino veritas "(there is) truth in wine," a proverbial expression

THE WAY OF THE WORLD

And that makes him so bright,
That he's able next morning to light us."

The sun's a good pimple,[50] an honest soaker; he has a
cellar at your Antipodes.[51] If I travel, aunt, I touch at your
Antipodes; your Antipodes are a good, rascally sort of
topsy-turvy fellows. If I had a bumper, I'd stand upon my
head and drink a health to 'em. A match or no match,
cousin with the hard name? Aunt, Wilfull will do't. If she
has her maidenhead, let her look to't; if she has not, let her
keep her own counsel in the meantime, and cry out at the
nine months' end.[52]

MRS. MIL. Your pardon, madam, I can stay no longer.
Sir Wilfull grows very powerful. Egh! how he smells! I
shall be overcome, if I stay. Come, cousin.

(*Exeunt* MRS. MILLAMANT *and* MRS. FAINALL.)

LADY WISH. Smells! he would poison a tallow-chandler[53]
and his family! Beastly creature, I know not what to do
with him! Travel, quotha! aye, travel, travel, get thee gone,
get thee but far enough, to the Saracens, or the Tartars,
or the Turks, for thou art not fit to live in a Christian
commonwealth, thou beastly pagan!

SIR WIL. Turks, no; no Turks, aunt: your Turks are in-
fidels, and believe not in the grape. Your Mahometan, your
Mussulman, is a dry stinkard.[54] No offence, aunt. My map
says that your Turk is not so honest a man as your Christian. I cannot find by the map that your mufti [55] is orthodox; whereby it is a plain case that orthodox is a hard
word, aunt, and (*hiccup*) Greek for claret.

---

[50] a good pimple a boon companion   [51] Antipodes the parts of
the globe diametrically opposite where we are; also, the people
who live there   [52] the nine months' end when a child will be
born   [53] tallow-chandler a maker or seller of tallow candles
[54] a dry stinkard a stinking, paltry fellow who does not drink;
referring to the Mahometan prohibition of wine and spirituous
liquors   [55] mufti official expounder of Moslem law

(Sings) "To drink is a Christian diversion,
Unknown to the Turk or the Persian:
　　Let Mahometan fools
　　Live by heathenish rules,
And be damned over tea-cups and coffee!
　　But let British lads sing,
　　Crown a health to the king,
And a fig for your sultan and sophy!" [56]

Ah, Tony!

(Enter FOIBLE, *and whispers* LADY WISHFORT)

LADY WISH. *(Aside to* FOIBLE) Sir Rowland impatient?
Good lack! what shall I do with this beastly tumbril? [57]
(Aloud) Go lie down and sleep, you sot! or, as I'm a person, I'll have you bastinadoed [58] with broomsticks. Call up
the wenches with broomsticks.　　　*(Exit* FOIBLE)

SIR WIL. Ahey! Wenches, where are the wenches?

LADY WISH. Dear Cousin Witwoud, get him away, and
you will bind me to you inviolably. I have an affair of moment that invades me with some precipitation. You will
oblige me to all futurity.

WIT. Come, knight. Pox on him, I don't know what to
say to him. Will you go to a cock-match?

SIR WIL. With a wench, Tony? Is she a shake-bag,[59]
Sirrah? Let me bite your cheek[60] for that.

WIT. Horrible! he has a breath like a bag-pipe! Aye, aye,
come, will you march, my Salopian?[61]

SIR WIL. Lead on, little Tony; I'll follow thee, my Anthony, my Tantony.[62] Sirrah, thou shalt be my Tantony,
and I'll be thy pig.

[56] sophy a former title of the kings of Persia　[57] tumbril a
farmer's cart　[58] bastinadoed beaten on the soles of the feet, as
m an Oriental form of punishment　[59] a shake-bag a gamecock of the largest size, i.e. a good subject for sport　[60] bite
your cheek give you a violent kiss, as a sign of affection
[61] Salopian an inhabitant of Shropshire　[62] Tantony a corruption
of "Saint Anthony" Saint Anthony was often represented as
being attended by a pig.

"And a fig for your sultan and sophy."

(*Exit singing with* WITWOUD)

LADY WISH. This will never do. It will never make a match; at least before he has been abroad.

(*Enter* WAITWELL, *disguised as* SIR ROWLAND)

Dear Sir Rowland, I am confounded with confusion at the retrospection of my own rudeness! I have more pardons to ask than the Pope distributes in the Year of Jubilee.[63] But I hope, where there is likely to be so near an alliance, we may unbend the severity of decorum and dispense with a little ceremony.

WAIT. My impatience, madam, is the effect of my transport; and till I have the possession of your adorable person, I am tantalized on the rack, and do but hang, madam, on the tenter[64] of expectation.

LADY WISH. You have excess of gallantry, Sir Rowland, and press things to a conclusion with a most prevailing vehemence. But a day or two for decency of marriage—

WAIT. For decency of funeral, madam! The delay will break my heart; or, if that should fail, I shall be poisoned. My nephew will get an inkling of my designs, and poison me; and I would willingly starve him before I die; I would gladly go out of the world with that satisfaction. That would be some comfort to me, if I could but live so long as to be revenged on that unnatural viper.

LADY WISH. Is he so unnatural, say you? Truly I would contribute much both to the saving of your life, and the accomplishment of your revenge. Not that I respect myself, though he has been a perfidious wretch to me.

WAIT. Perfidious to you!

LADY WISH. O Sir Rowland, the hours that he has died away at my feet, the tears that he has shed, the oaths that he has sworn, the palpitations that he has felt, the trances

[63] the Year of Jubilee the year in which the Pope proclaims remission of the entire temporal punishment that is ordinarily imposed for sin   [64] tenter a frame for stretching cloth; also, a tenter hook

and the tremblings, the ardours and the ecstacies, the kneelings and the risings, the heart-heavings and the hand-gripings, the pangs and the pathetic regards of his protesting eyes! Oh, no memory can register!

WAIT. What, my rival! Is the rebel my rival? 'A dies.

LADY WISH. No, don't kill him at once, Sir Rowland; starve him gradually, inch by inch.

WAIT. I'll do't. In three weeks he shall be barefoot; in a month out at knees with begging and alms. He shall starve upward and upward, till he has nothing living but his head, and then go out in a stink like a candle's end upon a save-all.[65]

LADY WISH. Well, Sir Rowland, you have the way. You are no novice in the labyrinth of love; you have the clue. But as I am a person, Sir Rowland, you must not attribute my yielding to any sinister appetite, or indigestion of widowhood; nor impute my complacency to any lethargy of continence. I hope you do not think me prone to any iteration[66] of nuptials.

WAIT. Far be it from me—

LADY WISH. If you do, I protest I must recede, or think that I have made a prostitution of decorums; but in the vehemence of compassion, and to save the life of a person of so much importance—

WAIT. I esteem it so.

LADY WISH. Or else you wrong my condescension.

WAIT. I do not, I do not!

LADY WISH. Indeed you do.

WAIT. I do not, fair shrine of virtue!

LADY WISH. If you think the least scruple of carnality[67] was an ingredient—

WAIT. Dear madam, no. You are all camphire[68] and frankincense, all chastity and odour.

LADY WISH. Or that—

(Re-enter FOIBLE)

[65] save-all a device in a candlestick to hold the ends of candles, so that they may be burned   [66] iteration repetition   [67] carnality sensuality   [68] camphire camphor, supposed to lessen sexual desire

Foib. Madam, the dancers are ready; and there's one with a letter, who must deliver it into your own hands.

Lady Wish. Sir Rowland, will you give me leave? Think favourably, judge candidly, and conclude you have found a person who would suffer racks in honour's cause, dear Sir Rowland, and will wait on you incessantly.[69]   (*Exit*)

Wait. Fie, fie! What a slavery have I undergone! Spouse, hast thou any cordial? I want spirits.

Foib. What a washy[70] rogue art thou, to pant thus for a quarter of an hour's lying and swearing to a fine lady!

Wait. Oh, she is the antidote to desire! Spouse, thou wilt fare the worse for't. I shall have no appetite to "iteration of nuptials" this eight-and-forty hours. By this hand I'd rather be a chair-man[71] in the dog-days[72] than act Sir Rowland till this time to-morrow!

(*Re-enter* Lady Wishfort, *with a letter*)

Lady Wish. Call in the dancers. Sir Rowland, we'll sit, if you please, and see the entertainment. (*Dance*) Now, with your permission, Sir Rowland, I will peruse my letter. I would open it in your presence, because I would not make you uneasy. If it should make you uneasy, I would burn it. Speak, if it does. But you may see by the superscription it is like a woman's hand.

Foib. (*Aside to* Waitwell) By Heaven! Mrs. Marwood's; I know it. My heart aches. Get it from her.

Wait. A woman's hand? No, madam, that's no woman's hand; I see that already. That's somebody whose throat must be cut.

Lady Wish. Nay, Sir Rowland, since you give me a proof of your passion by your jealousy, I promise you I'll make you a return, by a frank communication. You shall see it; we'll open it together. Look you here. (*Reads*) "Madam, though unknown to you." Look you there; 'tis

[69] incessantly instantly, immediately   [70] washy watery, weak
[71] chair-man a man whose business it is to carry people in a sedan chair   [72] the dog-days a period of from four to six weeks between early July and early September; the sultry, close part of the summer

from nobody that I know. "I have that honour for your character, that I think myself obliged to let you know you are abused. He who pretends to be Sir Rowland is a cheat and a rascal." Oh, heavens! what's this?

FOIB. (*Aside*) Unfortunate! all's ruined!

WAIT. How, how, let me see, let me see! (*reading*) "A rascal, and disguised and suborned [73] for that imposture." O villainy! O villainy! "by the contrivance of—"

LADY WISH. I shall faint, I shall die, I shall die, oh!

FOIB. (*Aside to* WAITWELL) Say 'tis your nephew's hand. Quickly, his plot, swear, swear it!

WAIT. Here's a villain! Madam, don't you perceive it? don't you see it?

LADY WISH. Too well, too well! I have seen too much.

WAIT. I told you at first I knew the hand. A woman's hand? The rascal writes a sort of a large hand, your Roman hand.[74] I saw there was a throat to be cut presently. If he were my son, as he is my nephew, I'd pistol him!

FOIB. Oh, treachery! But are you sure, Sir Rowland, it is his writing?

WAIT. Sure? Am I here? Do I live? Do I love this pearl of India? I have twenty letters in my pocket from him in the same character.[75]

LADY WISH. How!

FOIB. Oh, what luck it is, Sir Rowland, that you were present at this juncture! This was the business that brought Mr. Mirabell disguised to Madam Millamant this afternoon. I thought something was contriving, when he stole by me and would have hid his face.

LADY WISH. How, how! I heard the villain was in the house indeed; and now I remember, my niece went away abruptly, when Sir Wilfull was to have made his addresses.

FOIB. Then, then, madam, Mr. Mirabell waited for her in her chamber, but I would not tell your ladyship to discompose[76] you when you were to receive Sir Rowland.

WAIT. Enough, his date is short.

[73] **suborned** persuaded by bribery to commit a foul deed   [74] **Roman hand** round and bold handwriting   [75] **character** handwriting   [76] **discompose** agitate, upset

FOIB. No, good Sir Rowland, don't incur the law.

WAIT. Law? I care not for law. I can but die, and 'tis in a good cause. My lady shall be satisfied of my truth and innocence, though it cost me my life.

LADY WISH. No, dear Sir Rowland, don't fight; if you should be killed, I must never show my face, or hanged. Oh, consider my reputation, Sir Rowland! No, you shan't fight. I'll go in and examine my niece; I'll make her confess. I conjure you, Sir Rowland, by all your love, not to fight.

WAIT. I am charmed, madam; I obey. But some proof you must let me give you; I'll go for a black box, which contains the writings of my whole estate, and deliver that into your hands.

LADY WISH. Aye, dear Sir Rowland, that will be some comfort; bring the black box.

WAIT. And may I presume to bring a contract to be signed this night? May I hope so far?

LADY WISH. Bring what you will; but come alive, pray come alive. Oh, this is a happy discovery!

WAIT. Dead or alive I'll come, and married we will be in spite of treachery; aye, and get an heir that shall defeat the last remaining glimpse of hope in my abandoned nephew. Come, my buxom widow.

　　Ere long you shall substantial proof receive,

　　That I'm an arrant[77] knight—

FOIB. (*Aside*)　　　　　　　　　　Or arrant[78] knave.

　　　　　　　　　　　　　　　　　　　(*Exeunt*)

Act V

[*Scene continues*]

(*Enter* LADY WISHFORT *and* FOIBLE)

LADY WISH. Out of my house, out of my house, thou viper! thou serpent, that I have fostered! thou bosom traitress, that I raised from nothing! Begone! begone! begone!

[77] arrant errant, wandering　　[78] arrant pre-eminently bad

go! go! That I took from washing of old gauze and weaving of dead hair, with a bleak blue nose, over a chafing-dish of starved embers, and dining behind a travers rag,[1] in a shop no bigger than a birdcage! Go, go! starve again, do, do!

FOIB. Dear madam, I'll beg pardon on my knees.

LADY WISH. Away! out! out! Go set up for yourself again! Do, drive a trade, do, with your three-pennyworth of small ware flaunting upon a packthread,[2] under a brandy-seller's bulk,[3] or against a dead wall by a ballad-monger! Go, hang out an old frisoneer-gorget,[4] with a yard of yellow colberteen[5] again. Do; an old gnawed mask, two rows of pins, and a child's fiddle; a glass necklace with the beads broken, and a quilted nightcap with one ear. Go, go, drive a trade! These were your commodities, you treacherous trull! this was the merchandise you dealt in, when I took you into my house, placed you next myself, and made you governante[6] of my whole family! You have forgot this, have you, now you have feathered your nest?

FOIB. No, no, dear madam. Do but hear me; have but a moment's patience. I'll confess all. Mr. Mirabell seduced me; I am not the first that he has wheedled with his dissembling tongue. Your ladyship's own wisdom has been deluded by him; then how should I, a poor ignorant, defend myself? O madam, if you knew but what he promised me, and how he assured me your ladyship should come to no damage! Or else the wealth of the Indies should not have bribed me to conspire against so good, so sweet, so kind a lady as you have been to me.

LADY WISH. "No damage?" What, to betray me, to marry me to a cast-servingman?[7] to make me a receptacle, a

[1] travers rag a rag used as a traverse or screen [2] packthread strong thread or small twine [3] bulk projecting part of a building used for a booth in which business is conducted; cf. bulkhead [4] frisoneer-gorget a kind of covering for the neck and breast made of rough Frisian cloth [5] colberteen a kind of French lace, the making of which was encouraged by Colbert, a minister of Louis XIV. It was not highly esteemed in the England of Congreve's day. [6] governante housekeeper [7] a cast-servingman a discharged servant

hospital for a decayed pimp? "No damage?" O thou frontless[8] impudence, more than a big-bellied actress!

FOIB. Pray do but hear me, madam; he could not marry
your ladyship, madam. No indeed; his marriage was to
have been void in law, for he was married to me first, to
secure your ladyship. He could not have bedded your
ladyship; for if he had consummated with your ladyship,
he must have run the risk of the law[9] and been put upon
his clergy.[10] Yes indeed; I inquired of the law in that case
before I would meddle or make.[11]

LADY WISH. What, then I have been your property, have
I? I have been convenient to you, it seems! While you were
catering for Mirabell, I have been broker[12] for you? What,
have you made a passive bawd of me? This exceeds all
precedent; I am brought to fine uses, to become a botcher[13]
of second-hand marriages between Abigails and Andrews! [14] I'll couple you! Yes, I'll baste you together, you
and your Philander! [15] I'll Duke's-Place you, as I'm a person!
Your turtle is in custody already; you shall coo in the same
cage, if there be a constable or warrant in the parish. (*Exit*)

FOIB. Oh, that ever I was born! Oh, that I was ever
married! A bride! aye, I shall be a Bridewell-bride.[16] Oh!

(*Enter* MRS. FAINALL)

MRS. FAIN. Poor Foible, what's the matter?

[8] frontless shameless   [9] run the risk of the law i.e. for bigamy
[10] been put upon his clergy claimed the benefit of clergy, origin-
ally an exemption of clergymen from trial by a secular court,
a privilege later extended to all *clerici*, or clerks, i.e. those
who could read   [11] meddle or make intrude into another's
private concerns. "Meddle and make" was a colloquial phrase.
[12] broker a marriage broker   [13] botcher mender or patcher
[14] Abigails and Andrews waiting-maids and menservants, from
characters in Beaumont and Fletcher's *The Scornful Lady* and
The Elder Brother respectively   [15] Philander lover, from a
character in Beaumont and Fletcher's *The Laws of Candy*.
Beaumont and Fletcher seem to have been favorite authors of
Lady Wishfort's.   [16] a Bridewell-bride a bride in Bridewell
Prison, a house of correction, where disreputable women were
often punished by being made to beat hemp

FOIB. O madam, my lady's gone for a constable. I shall be had to a justice, and put to Bridewell to beat hemp. Poor Waitwell's gone to prison already.

MRS. FAIN. Have a good heart, Foible; Mirabell's gone to give security[17] for him. This is all Marwood's and my husband's doing.

FOIB. Yes, yes, I know it, madam; she was in my lady's closet, and overheard all that you said to me before dinner. She sent the letter to my lady; and that missing effect, Mr. Fainall laid this plot to arrest Waitwell, when he pretended to go for the papers; and in the meantime Mrs. Marwood declared all to my lady.

MRS. FAIN. Was there no mention made of me in the letter? My mother does not suspect my being in the confederacy? I fancy Marwood has not told her, though she has told my husband.

FOIB. Yes, madam; but my lady did not see that part. We stifled the letter before she read so far. Has that mischievous devil told Mr. Fainall of your ladyship then?

MRS. FAIN. Aye, all's out, my affair with Mirabell, everything discovered. This is the last day of our living together; that's my comfort.

FOIB. Indeed, madam, and so 'tis a comfort if you knew all. He has been even with your ladyship;[18] which I could have told you long enough since, but I love to keep peace and quietness by my good will. I had rather bring friends together than set 'em at distance. But Mrs. Marwood and he are nearer related than ever their parents thought for.

MRS. FAIN. Sayest thou so, Foible? Canst thou prove this?

FOIB. I can take my oath on it, madam; so can Mrs. Mincing. We have had many a fair word from Madam Marwood, to conceal something that passed in our chamber one evening when you were at Hyde Park and we were thought to have gone a-walking; but we went up unawares, though we were sworn to secrecy too. Madam Marwood took a book and swore us upon it, but it was a book of

[17] security bail   [18] He has been even with your ladyship Fainall has got even with his wife for her past affair with Mirabell·by his own present affair with Mrs. Marwood.

verses and poems. So as long is it was not a Bible oath, we may break it with a safe conscience.

MRS. FAIN. This discovery is the most opportune thing I could wish. Now, Mincing?

(*Enter* MINCING)

MIN. My lady[19] would speak with Mrs. Foible, mem. Mr. Mirabell is with her; he has set your spouse at liberty, Mrs. Foible, and would have you hide yourself in my lady's closet till my old lady's anger is abated. Oh, my old lady is in a perilous passion at something Mr. Fainall has said; he swears, and my old lady cries. There's a fearful hurricane, I vow. He says, mem, how that he'll have my lady's fortune made over to him, or he'll be divorced.

MRS. FAIN. Does your lady or Mirabell know that?

MIN. Yes, mem; they have sent me to see if Sir Wilfull be sober and to bring him to them. My lady is resolved to have him, I think, rather than lose such a vast sum as six thousand pound. Oh, come, Mrs. Foible, I hear my old lady.

MRS. FAIN. Foible, you must tell Mincing that she must prepare to vouch[20] when I call her.

FOIB. Yes, yes, madam.

MIN. O yes, mem, I'll vouch anything for your ladyship's service, be what it will.   (*Exeunt* MINCING *and* FOIBLE)

(*Re-enter* LADY WISHFORT, *with* MRS. MARWOOD)

LADY WISH. O my dear friend, how can I enumerate the benefits that I have received from your goodness? To you I owe the timely discovery of the false vows of Mirabell; to you I owe the detection of the impostor Sir Rowland. And now you are become an intercessor with my son-in-law, to save the honour of my house, and compound for the frailties of my daughter. Well, friend, you are enough to reconcile me to the bad world, or else I would retire to deserts and solitudes, and feed harmless sheep by groves

[19] My lady i.e. Mrs. Millamant. Mincing is Millamant's maid.
[20] vouch give evidence

and purling[21] streams. Dear Marwood, let us leave the world, and retire by ourselves and be shepherdesses.

MRS. MAR. Let us first dispatch the affair at hand, madam. We shall have leisure to think of retirement afterwards. Here is one who is concerned in the treaty.

LADY WISH. O daughter, daughter, is it possible thou shouldst be my child, bone of my bone, and flesh of my flesh, and, as I may say, another me, and yet transgress the most minute particle of severe virtue? Is it possible you should lean aside to iniquity, who have been cast in the direct mould of virtue? I have not only been a mould but a pattern for you, and a model for you, after you were brought into the world.

MRS. FAIN. I don't understand your ladyship.

LADY WISH. Not understand? Why, have you not been naught? [22] have you not been sophisticated? [23] Not understand? Here I am ruined to compound [24] for your caprices and your cuckoldoms. I must pawn my plate and my jewels, and ruin my niece, and all little enough.

MRS. FAIN. I am wronged and abused, and so are you. 'Tis a false accusation, as false as hell, as false as your friend there, aye, or your friend's friend, my false husband.

MRS. MAR. My friend, Mrs. Fainall? Your husband my friend? What do you mean?

MRS. FAIN. I know what I mean, madam, and so do you; and so shall the world at a time convenient.

MRS. MAR. I am sorry to see you so passionate, madam. More temper[25] would look more like innocence. But I have done. I am sorry my zeal to serve your ladyship and family should admit of misconstruction, or make me liable to affronts. You will pardon me, madam, if I meddle no more with an affair in which I am not personally concerned.

LADY WISH. O dear friend, I am so ashamed that you should meet with such returns! (*To* MRS. FAINALL) You ought to ask pardon on your knees, ungrateful creature;

[21] purling murmuring   [22] naught naughty, wicked   [23] sophisticated deprived of original innocence   [24] compound make composition, a payment to prevent prosecution for an offense   [25] temper temperateness

she deserves more from you than all your life can accomplish. (*To* MRS. MARWOOD) Oh, don't leave me destitute in this perplexity! No, stick to me, my good genius.

MRS. FAIN. I tell you, madam, you're abused. Stick to you? Aye, like a leech, to suck your best blood; she'll drop off when she's full. Madam, you shan't pawn a bodkin,[26] nor part with a brass counter,[27] in composition for me. I defy 'em all. Let 'em prove their aspersions; I know my own innocence, and dare stand a trial.   (*Exit*)

LADY WISH. Why, if she should be innocent, if she should be wronged after all, ha? I don't know what to think; and, I promise you, her education has been unexceptionable.[28] I may say it; for I chiefly made it my own care to initiate her very infancy in the rudiments of virtue, and to impress upon her tender years a young odium[29] and aversion to the very sight of men. Aye, friend, she would ha' shrieked if she had but seen a man, till she was in her teens. As I'm a person 'tis true. She was never suffered to play with a male child, though but in coats; nay, her very babies[30] were of the feminine gender. Oh, she never looked a man in the face but her own father, or the chaplain, and him we made a shift[31] to put upon her for a woman, by the help of his long garments and his sleek face, till she was going in her fifteen.[32]

MRS. MAR. 'Twas much she should be deceived so long.

LADY WISH. I warrant you, or she would never have borne to have been catechized by him; and have heard his long lectures against singing and dancing, and such debaucheries, and going to filthy plays, and profane music-meetings, where the lewd trebles squeak nothing but bawdy, and the basses roar blasphemy. Oh, she would have swooned at the sight or name of an obscene play-book! And can I think, after all this, that my daughter can be naught? What, a whore? and thought it excommunication to set

[26] **a bodkin** a large-eyed blunt needle, or a kind of pin used by women to fasten their hair [27] **a brass counter** a coin of base metal used as a token of payment [28] **unexceptionable** beyond reproach [29] **odium** hatred [30] **babies** dolls [31] **made a shift** used a trick [32] **going in her fifteen** going into her fifteenth year

her foot within the door of a playhouse! O my dear friend, I can't believe it, no, no! As she says, let him prove it, let him prove it.

MRS. MAR. Prove it, madam? What, and have your name prostituted in a public court? yours and your daughter's reputation worried at the bar by a pack of bawling lawyers? To be ushered in with an *O yes*[33] of scandal, and have your case opened by an old fumbling lecher in a quoif [34] like a man-midwife; to bring your daughter's infamy to light; to be a theme for legal punsters and quibblers by the statute, and become a jest against a rule of court, where there is no precedent for a jest in any record, not even in Doomsday Book;[35] to discompose the gravity of the bench, and provoke naughty interrogatories in more naughty law Latin, while the good judge, tickled with the proceeding, simpers under a grey beard, and fidges[36] off and on his cushion as if he had swallowed cantharides,[37] or sat upon cow-itch! [38]

LADY WISH. Oh, 'tis very hard!

MRS. MAR. And then to have my young revellers of the Temple[39] take notes, like prentices at a conventicle;[40] and after, talk it all over again in commons,[41] or before drawers in an eating-house.

LADY WISH. Worse and worse!

MRS. MAR. Nay, this is nothing; if it would end here, 'twere well. But it must, after this, be consigned by the shorthand writers to the public press; and from thence be

---

[33] O yes Oyez, "Hear ye," a cry used by court-criers to secure silence before making a proclamation   [34] quoif coif, a white cap formerly worn by English lawyers   [35] Doomsday Book the record of a great survey of the lands of England made in 1085-86, by order of William the Conqueror   [36] fidges fidgets   [37] cantharides a preparation of dried beetles used for medicinal purposes   [38] cow-itch cowhage, a tropical vine having pods covered with barbed hairs which cause violent itching   [39] the Temple The Inner and Middle Temple were two of the four Inns of Court.   [40] take notes, like prentices at a conventicle indentured apprentices were supposed to take notes on the sermon in a meetinghouse for the use of their employers   [41] commons the dining hall of a collegiate institution

transferred to the hands, nay into the throats and lungs of hawkers,[42] with voices more licentious than the loud flounder-man's,[43] or the woman that cries grey peas. And this you must hear till you are stunned; nay, you must hear nothing else for some days.

LADY WISH. Oh, 'tis insupportable! No, no, dear friend; make it up, make it up; aye, aye, I'll compound. I'll give up all, myself and my all, my niece and her all, anything, everything for composition.

MRS. MAR. Nay, madam, I advise nothing; I only lay before you, as a friend, the inconveniences which perhaps you have overseen. Here comes Mr. Fainall; if he will be satisfied to huddle up all in silence, I shall be glad. You must think I would rather congratulate than condole with you.

(*Enter* FAINALL)

LADY WISH. Aye, aye, I do not doubt it, dear Marwood; no, no, I do not doubt it.

FAIN. Well, madam, I have suffered myself to be overcome by the importunity of this lady your friend, and am content you shall enjoy your own proper estate during life, on condition you oblige yourself never to marry, under such penalty as I think convenient.

LADY WISH. Never to marry?

FAIN. No more Sir Rowlands; the next imposture may not be so timely detected.

MRS. MAR. That condition, I dare answer, my lady will consent to, without difficulty; she has already but too much experienced the perfidiousness of men. Besides, madam, when we retire to our pastoral solitude, we shall bid adieu to all other thoughts.

LADY WISH. Aye, that's true; but in case of necessity, as of health, or some such emergency——

FAIN. Oh, if you are prescribed marriage, you shall be considered; I will only reserve to myself the power to choose for you. If your physic be wholesome, it matters

[42] hawkers peddlers   [43] the loud flounder-man's There was a well-known crier of flounders in the streets of London whose voice was loud and unrestrained.

not who is your apothecary. Next, my wife shall settle on
me the remainder of her fortune, not made over already;
and for her maintenance depend entirely on my discretion.

LADY WISH. This is most inhumanly savage, exceeding
the barbarity of a Muscovite[44] husband.

FAIN. I learned it from his Czarish majesty's retinue,[45]
in a winter evening's conference over brandy and pepper,
amongst other secrets of matrimony and policy, as they
are at present practised in the northern hemisphere. But
this must be agreed unto, and that positively. Lastly, I
will be endowed, in right of my wife, with that six thousand pound, which is the moiety of Mrs. Millamant's fortune in your possession; and which she has forfeited (as
will appear by the last will and testament of your deceased
husband, Sir Jonathan Wishfort) by her disobedience in
contracting herself against your consent or knowledge, and
by refusing the offered match with Sir Wilfull Witwoud,
which you, like a careful aunt, had provided for her.

LADY WISH. My nephew was *non compos*,[46] and could
not make his addresses.

FAIN. I come to make demands. I'll hear no objections.

LADY WISH. You will grant me time to consider?

FAIN. Yes, while the instrument[47] is drawing, to which
you must set your hand till more sufficient deeds can be
perfected; which I will take care shall be done with all
possible speed. In the meanwhile I will go for the said
instrument, and till my return you may balance this matter
in your own discretion.   (*Exit*)

LADY WISH. This insolence is beyond all precedent, all
parallel; must I be subject to this merciless villain?

MRS. MAR. 'Tis severe indeed, madam, that you should
smart for your daughter's wantonness.

LADY WISH. 'Twas against my consent that she married
this barbarian, but she would have him, though her year[48]
was not out. Ah! her first husband, my son Languish,

Muscovite Russian **his Czarish majesty's retinue** Peter the
Great had visited England early in 1698. **non compos** not
in his right senses **instrument** legal document **her year**
of formal mourning

would not have carried it thus.[49] Well, that was my choice,
this is hers; she is matched now with a witness.[50] I shall
be mad! Dear friend, is there no comfort for me? must I
live to be confiscated [51] at this rebel-rate? [52] Here come
two more of my Egyptian plagues[53] too.

(*Enter* MRS. MILLAMANT *and* SIR WILFULL WITWOUD)

SIR WIL. Aunt, your servant.

LADY WISH. Out, caterpillar, call not me aunt! I know
thee not!

SIR WIL. I confess I have been a little in disguise,[54] as
they say. 'Sheart! and I'm sorry for't. What would you
have? I hope I committed no offence, aunt, and if I did,
I am willing to make satisfaction; and what can a man say
fairer? If I have broke anything, I'll pay for't, an it cost
a pound. And so let that content for what's past, and make
no more words. For what's to come, to pleasure you I'm
willing to marry my cousin. So pray let's all be friends;
she and I are agreed upon the matter before a witness.

LADY WISH. How's this, dear niece? Have I any comfort? Can this be true?

MRS. MIL. I am content to be a sacrifice to your repose,
madam; and to convince you that I had no hand in the
plot, as you were misinformed, I have laid my commands
on Mirabell to come in person, and be a witness that I
give my hand to this flower of knighthood; and for the
contract that passed between Mirabell and me, I have
obliged him to make a resignation of it in your ladyship's
presence. He is without, and waits your leave for admit-
tance.

LADY WISH. Well, I'll swear I am something revived at
this testimony of your obedience; but I cannot admit that
traitor. I fear I cannot fortify myself to support his appear-

---

[49] carried it thus acted like this   [50] with a witness effectually,
with great force   [51] be confiscated have one's property seized
[52] at this rebel-rate in this rebellious, high-handed manner
[53] two more of my Egyptian plagues a reference to the ten
plagues of Egypt cf. *Exodus* VII-XII   [54] in disguise not my
natural self, intoxicated

ance. He is as terrible to me as a Gorgon;[55] if I see him, I fear I shall turn to stone, petrify incessantly.

MRS. MIL. If you disoblige him, he may resent your refusal, and insist upon the contract still. Then 'tis the last time he will be offensive to you.

LADY WISH. Are you sure it will be the last time? If I were sure of that! Shall I never see him again?

MRS. MIL. Sir Wilfull, you and he are to travel together, are you not?

SIR WIL. 'Sheart, the gentleman's a civil gentleman, aunt; let him come in. Why, we are sworn brothers and fellow-travellers. We are to be Pylades and Orestes,[56] he and I. He is to be my interpreter in foreign parts. He has been overseas once already; and with *proviso* that I marry my cousin, will cross 'em once again, only to bear me company. 'Sheart, Ill call him in. An I set on't once,[57] he shall come in; and see who'll hinder him.   (*Exit*)

MRS. MAR. This is precious fooling, if it would pass; but I'll know the bottom of it.

LADY WISH. O dear Marwood, you are not going?

MRS. MAR. Not far, madam; I'll return immediately.
                                                    (*Exit*)

(*Re-enter* SIR WILFULL *with* MIRABELL)

SIR WIL. Look up, man, I'll stand by you; 'sbud an she do frown, she can't kill you; besides, harkee, she dare not frown desperately, because her face is none of her own. 'Sheart, an she should, her forehead would wrinkle like the coat of a cream-cheese; but mum for that, fellow-traveller.

MIR. If a deep sense of the many injuries I have offered to so good a lady, with a sincere remorse and a hearty contrition, can but obtain the least glance of compassion, I am too happy. Ah, madam, there was a time! But let

[55] **Gorgon** one of the three snaky-haired sisters whose hideous appearance turned the beholder to stone [56] **Pylades and Orestes** Pylades was the faithful friend of Orestes, son of Agamemnon and Clytemnestra [57] **An I set on't once** if I once set my heart on it

it be forgotten. I confess I have deservedly forfeited the high place I once held, of sighing at your feet. Nay, kill me not, by turning from me in disdain. I come not to plead for favour; nay, not for pardon. I am a suppliant only for your pity. I am going where I never shall behold you more.

SIR WIL. How, fellow-traveller! You shall go by yourself then.

MIR. Let me be pitied first, and afterwards forgotten. I ask no more.

SIR WIL. By'r lady, a very reasonable request, and will cost you nothing, aunt. Come, come, forgive and forget, aunt; why you must, an you are a Christian.

MIR. Consider, madam, in reality you could not receive much prejudice; it was an innocent device, though I confess it had a face of guiltiness. It was at most an artifice which love contrived, and errors which love produces have ever been accounted venial. At least think it is punishment enough that I have lost what in my heart I hold most dear, that to your cruel indignation I have offered up this beauty, and with her my peace and quiet; nay, all my hopes of future comfort.

SIR WIL. An he does not move me, would I may never be o' the quorum! [58] An it were not as good a deed as to drink, to give her to him again, I would never take shipping! Aunt, if you don't forgive quickly, I shall melt, I can tell you that. My contract went no farther than a little mouth-glue, and that's hardly dry; one doleful sigh more from my fellow-traveller, and 'tis dissolved.

LADY WISH. Well, nephew, upon your account—ah, he has a false insinuating tongue! Well, sir, I will stifle my just resentment at my nephew's request. I will endeavour what I can to forget, but on *proviso* that you resign the contract with my niece immediately.

MIR. It is in writing, and with papers of concern; but I have sent my servant for it, and will deliver it to you, with all acknowledgments for your transcendent goodness.

[58] the quorum the justices of the peace collectively

WILLIAM CONGREVE

LADY WISH. (*Aside*) Oh, he has witchcraft in his eyes and tongue! When I did not see him, I could have bribed a villain to his assassination; but his appearance rakes the embers which have so long lain smothered in my breast.

(*Re-enter* FAINALL *and* MRS. MARWOOD)

FAIN. Your date of deliberation, madam, is expired. Here is the instrument; are you prepared to sign?

LADY WISH. If I were prepared, I am not empowered. My niece exerts a lawful claim, having matched herself by my direction to Sir Wilfull.

FAIN. That sham is too gross to pass on me, though 'tis imposed on you, madam.

MRS. MIL. Sir, I have given my consent.

MIR. And, sir, I have resigned my pretensions.

SIR WIL. And, sir, I assert my right; and will maintain it in defiance of you, sir, and of your instrument. 'Sheart, an you talk of an instrument, sir, I have an old fox[59] by my thigh shall hack your instrument of ram vellum[60] to shreds, sir! It shall not be sufficient for a *mittimus*[61] or a tailor's measure.[62] Therefore withdraw your instrument, sir, or, by'r lady, I shall draw mine.

LADY WISH. Hold, nephew, hold!

MRS. MIL. Good Sir Wilfull, respite[63] your valour.

FAIN. Indeed? Are you provided of your guard, with your single beef-eater[64] there? But I'm prepared for you, and insist upon my first proposal. You shall submit your own estate to my management and absolutely make over my wife's to my sole use, as pursuant to the purport and tenor of this other covenant. (*To* MRS. MILLAMANT) I suppose, madam, your consent is not requisite in this case; nor, Mr. Mirabell, your resignation; nor, Sir Wilfull, your right. You may draw your fox if you please, sir, and

---

[59] **fox** a kind of sword   [60] **ram vellum** parchment prepared from sheepskin   [61] **a mittimus** a warrant of commitment to prison   [62] **a tailor's measure** parchment used by tailors in taking measurements   [63] **respite** delay   [64] **beef-eater** a yeoman of the royal guard

make a Bear-Garden[65] flourish somewhere else; for here it will not avail. This, my Lady Wishfort, must be subscribed, or your darling daughter's turned adrift, like a leaky hulk, to sink or swim, as she and the current of this lewd town can agree.

LADY WISH. Is there no means, no remedy to stop my ruin? Ungrateful wretch! dost thou not owe thy being, thy subsistence, to my daughter's fortune?

FAIN. I'll answer you when I have the rest of it in my possession.

MIR. (*To* LADY WISHFORT) But that you would not accept of a remedy from my hands—I own I have not deserved you should owe any obligation to me; or else perhaps I could advise—

LADY WISH. Oh, what? what? to save me and my child from ruin, from want, I'll forgive all that's past; nay, I'll consent to anything to come, to be delivered from this tyranny.

MIR. Aye, madam, but that is too late; my reward is intercepted. You have disposed of her who only could have made me a compensation for all my services. But be it as it may, I am resolved I'll serve you; you shall not be wronged in this savage manner.

LADY WISH. How! Dear Mr. Mirabell, can you be so generous at last? But it is not possible. Harkee, I'll break my nephew's match; you shall have my niece yet, and all her fortune, if you can but save me from this imminent danger.

MIR. Will you? I take you at your word. I ask no more. I must have leave for two criminals to appear.

LADY WISH. Aye, aye; anybody, anybody!

MIR. Foible is one, and a penitent.

(*Re-enter* MRS. FAINALL, FOIBLE, *and* MINCING)

MRS. MAR. O my shame! (MIRABELL *and* LADY WISHFORT *go to* MRS. FAINALL *and* FOIBLE) These corrupt things are bought and brought hither to expose me.

(*To* FAINALL)

---

[65] Bear-Garden place for baiting bears; a scene of rowdiness

FAIN. If it must all come out, why let 'em know it; 'tis but *the way of the world*. That shall not urge me to relinquish or abate one tittle[66] of my terms; no, I will insist the more.

FOIB. Yes indeed, madam; I'll take my Bible-oath of it.

MIN. And so will I, mem.

LADY WISH. O Marwood. Marwood, art thou false? my friend deceive me? Hast thou been a wicked accomplice with that profligate man?

MRS. MAR. Have you so much ingratitude and injustice, to give credit against your friend to the aspersions of two such mercenary trulls?

MIN. "Mercenary," mem? I scorn your words. 'Tis true we found you and Mr. Fainall in the blue garret; by the same token, you swore us to secrecy upon Messalina's poems.[67] "Mercenary?" No, if we would have been mercenary, we should have held our tongues; you would have bribed us sufficiently.

FAIN. Go, you are an insignificant thing! Well, what are you the better for this? Is this Mr. Mirabell's expedient? I'll be put off no longer. You thing, that was a wife, shall smart for this! I will not leave thee wherewithal to hide thy shame; your body shall be naked as your reputation.

MRS. FAIN. I despise you, and defy your malice! You have aspersed me wrongfully. I have proved your falsehood. Go you and your treacherous—I will not name it, but starve together, perish!

FAIN. Not while you are worth a groat,[68] indeed, my dear. Madam, I'll be fooled no longer.

LADY WISH. Ah, Mr. Mirabell, this is small comfort, the detection of this affair.

MIR. Oh, in good time. Your leave for the other offender and penitent to appear, madam.

(*Enter* WAITWELL, *with a box of writings*)

---

[66] tittle a very small part   [67] Messalina's poems Messalina was the dissolute wife of the Roman emperor, Claudius. "Messalina's" is probably an error of Mincing's for "miscellaneous."
[68] groat an old English coin worth fourpence

LADY WISH. O Sir Rowland! Well, rascal?

WAIT. What your ladyship pleases. I have brought the black box at last, madam.

MIR. Give it me. Madam, you remember your promise.

LADY WISH. Aye, dear sir.

MIR. Where are the gentlemen?

WAIT. At hand, sir, rubbing their eyes; just risen from sleep.

FAIN. 'Sdeath, what's this to me? I'll not wait your private concerns.

(*Enter* PETULANT *and* WITWOUD)

PET. How now? What's the matter? Whose hand's out? [69]

WIT. Heyday! what, are you all got together, like players at the end of the last act?

MIR. You may remember, gentlemen, I once requested your hands as witnesses to a certain parchment.

WIT. Aye, I do; my hand I remember. Petulant set his mark.

MIR. You wrong him, his name is fairly written, as shall appear. You do not remember, gentlemen, anything of what that parchment contained?   (*Undoing the box*)

WIT. No.

PET. Not I. I writ. I read nothing.

MIR. Very well; now you shall know. Madam, your promise.

LADY WISH. Aye, aye, sir, upon my honour.

MIR. Mr. Fainall, it is now time that you should know that your lady, while she was at her own disposal, and before you had by your insinuations wheedled her out of a pretended settlement of the greatest part of her fortune—

FAIN. Sir! pretended!

MIR. Yes, sir. I say that this lady, while a widow, having it seems received some cautions respecting your inconstancy and tyranny of temper, which from her own

** Whose hand's out? Who is making trouble?

partial opinion and fondness of you she could never have suspected—she did, I say, by the wholesome advice of friends and of sages learned in the laws of this land, deliver this same as her act and deed to me in trust, and to the uses within mentioned. You may read if you please (*holding out the parchment*), though perhaps what is inscribed on the back may serve your occasions.

FAIN. Very likely, sir. What's here? Damnation! (*reads*) "A deed of conveyance of the whole estate real of Arabella Languish, widow, in trust to Edward Mirabell." Confusion!

MIR. Even so, sir; 'tis the *way of the world*, sir, of the widows of the world. I suppose this deed may bear an elder[70] date than what you have obtained from your lady?

FAIN. Perfidious fiend! then thus I'll be revenged.

(*Offers to run at* MRS. FAINALL)

SIR WIL. Hold, sir! Now you may make your Bear-Garden flourish somewhere else, sir.

FAIN. Mirabell, you shall hear of this, sir; be sure you shall. Let me pass, oaf!   (*Exit*)

MRS. FAIN. Madam, you seem to stifle your resentment; you had better give it vent.

MRS. MAR. Yes, it shall have vent, and to your confusion; or I'll perish in the attempt.   (*Exit*)

LADY WISH. O daughter, daughter, 'tis plain thou hast inherited thy mother's prudence.

MRS. FAIN. Thank Mr. Mirabell, a cautious friend, to whose advice all is owing.

LADY WISH. Well, Mr. Mirabell, you have kept your promise, and I must perform mine. First, I pardon, for your sake, Sir Rowland there, and Foible. The next thing is to break the matter to my nephew, and how to do that—

MIR. For that, madam, give yourself no trouble; let me have your consent. Sir Wilfull is my friend; he has had compassion upon lovers, and generously engaged a

[70] elder earlier

volunteer[71] in this action, for our service, and now designs to prosecute his travels.

SIR WIL. 'Sheart, aunt, I have no mind to marry. My cousin's a fine lady, and the gentleman loves her, and she loves him, and they deserve one another; my resolution is to see foreign parts. I have set on't, and when I'm set on't, I must do't. And if these two gentlemen would travel too, I think they may be spared.

PET. For my part, I say little; I think things are best off or on.[72]

WIT. I gad,[73] I understand nothing of the matter; I'm in a maze yet, like a dog in a dancing-school.

LADY WISH. Well, sir, take her, and with her all the joy I can give you.

MRS. MIL. Why does not the man take me? Would you have me give myself to you over again?

MIR. Aye, and over and over again; (*Kisses her hand*) for I would have you as often as possibly I can. Well, Heaven grant I love you not too well; that's all my fear.

SIR WIL. 'Sheart, you'll have time enough to toy[74] after you're married; or if you will toy now, let us have a dance in the meantime, that we who are not lovers may have some other employment besides looking on.

MIR. With all my heart, dear Sir Wilfull. What shall we do for music?

FOIB. Oh, sir, some that were provided for Sir Rowland's entertainment are yet within call.   (*A dance*)

LADY WISH. As I am a person, I can hold out no longer. I have wasted my spirits so to-day already that I am ready to sink under the fatigue; and I cannot but have some fears upon me yet that my son[75] Fainall will pursue some desperate course.

MIR. Madam, disquiet not yourself on that account; to my knowledge his circumstances are such, he must of force[76] comply.[77] For my part, I will contribute all that

[71] engaged a volunteer volunteered to take part   [72] off or on either way   [73] I gad Egad, i.e. by God   [74] toy play   [75] my son i.e. my son-in-law   [76] of force necessarily   [77] comply acquiesce

in me lies to a reunion; in the meantime, madam, (*To* MRS. FAINALL) let me before these witnesses restore to you this deed of trust; it may be a means, well-managed, to make you live easily together.

From hence let those be warned, who mean to wed,
Lest mutual falsehood stain the bridal bed;
For each deceiver to his cost may find,
That marriage-frauds too oft are paid in kind.

(Exeunt omnes)

EPILOGUE

SPOKEN BY MRS. BRACEGIRDLE[1]

After our Epilogue this crowd dismisses,
I'm thinking how this play'll be pulled to pieces.
But pray consider, ere you doom its fall,
How hard a thing 'twould be to please you all.
There are some critics so with spleen diseased,
They scarcely come inclining to be pleased;
And sure he must have more than mortal skill,
Who pleases any one against his will.
Then, all bad poets we are sure are foes,
And how their number's swelled, the town well knows;
In shoals I've marked 'em judging in the pit;
Though they're on no pretence for judgment fit,
But that they have been damned for want of wit.
Since when, they, by their own offences taught,
Set up for spies on plays, and finding fault.
Others there are whose malice we'd prevent;
Such who watch plays with scurrilous intent
To mark out who by characters are meant.
And though no perfect likeness they can trace,
Yet each pretends to know the copied face.
These with false glosses[2] feed their own ill nature,[3]
And turn to libel what was meant a satire.
May such malicious fops this fortune find,
To think themselves alone the fools designed;
If any are so arrogantly vain,
To think they singly[4] can support a scene,
And furnish fool enough[5] to entertain.

---

[1] **Mrs. Bracegirdle** Mrs. Anne Bracegirdle, one of the loves o
Congreve's life, played the part of Mrs. Millamant in *The War*
of the World. [2] **glosses** notes of explanation [3] **nature** pro-
nounced "nater" to rhyme with satire, "sater" [4] **singly** alone
[5] **furnish fool enough** furnish enough of a fool

For well the learned and the judicious know
That satire scorns to stoop so meanly low
As any one abstracted [6] fop to show.
For, as when painters form a matchless face,
They from each fair one catch some different grace;
And shining features in one portrait blend,
To which no single beauty must pretend;
So poets oft do in one piece expose
Whole *belles assemblées*[7] of *coquettes* and *beaux*.

[6] abstracted separated from others   [7] belles assemblées fashion-able gatherings

BIBLIOGRAPHY

BIOGRAPHY

Gosse, Edmund, *Life of William Congreve* (New York, 1924).

Hodges, John C., *William Congreve, the Man* (New York, 1941).

Taylor, D. Crane, *William Congreve* (London, 1931).

NINETEENTH-CENTURY CRITICISM

Hazlitt, William, "On Wycherley, Congreve, Vanbrugh and Farquhar," Lecture IV in *Lectures on the English Comic Writers*, 1819.

Lamb, Charles, "On the Artificial Comedy of the Last Century" in *Essays of Elia*, 1823.

Hunt, Leigh, Biographical and Critical Notices, prefixed to his edition of *The Dramatic Works of Wycherley, Congreve, Vanbrugh, and Farquhar*, 1840.

Macaulay, Thomas Babington, "Leigh Hunt's *Comic Dramatists of the Restoration*" in *Historical Essays*, 1843.

Thackeray, William Makepeace, "Congreve and Addison" Lecture II in *The English Humourists of the Eighteenth Century*, 1853.

Meredith, George, *An Essay on Comedy and the Uses of the Comic Spirit*, 1897.

TWENTIETH-CENTURY STUDIES

Dobrée, Bonamy, *Restoration Comedy, 1660-1720* (Oxford, 1924).

Palmer, John, *The Comedy of Manners* (London, 1913).

Perry, Henry Ten Eyck, *The Comic Spirit in Restoration Drama* (New Haven, 1925).

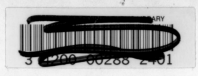

3/92

NEW HANOVER COUNTY PUBLIC LIBRARY
201 Chestnut Street
Wilmington, NC 28401